636 Kur

636 Kur

THE **Flymo** BOOK OF GARDEN GAMES & LAWN LEISURE

Carol Kurrein

Foreword by
Alan Titchmarsh

A Graham Tarrant Book
David & Charles

Newton Abbot   London   North Pomfret (Vt)

For Ben and Lucy

British Library Cataloguing in Publication Data

Kurrein, Carol
  The Flymo book of garden games &
  lawn leisure
  1. Gardens. Lawns
  I. Title
  635.9'647

  ISBN 0-7153-9339-1

Book designed by Michael Head

Typeset by Typesetters (Birmingham) Limited
Smethwick, West Midlands
and printed in Portugal
for David & Charles Publishers plc
Brunel House   Newton Abbot   Devon

Published in the United States of America
by David & Charles Inc
North Pomfret   Vermont 05053   USA

CONTENTS

FOREWORD

What a refreshing change! A book that actually encourages you to enjoy yourself in the garden. I'm a keen gardener and an enthusiastic plantsman, but with two children and three large dogs I'm forever gritting my teeth and trying hard to compromise.

After all, what's the point in having a museum of a garden where the greensward is to be looked at and never played on?

During the summer I go out looking at all sorts of gardens, from those behind tiny terrace houses, to those that surround stately homes and which were designed by the likes of Capability Brown and Humphry Repton.

Regardless of size, the ones that really appeal are those that show the evidence of tender loving care, but also of being lived in.

I want my children to grow up with a love of plants and gardens, not a fear of them, and they get a great kick out of paddling pools and tree houses and dens.

Carol Kurrein's book makes sure you have your priorities right. She'll tell you how to make a good lawn, and how to keep it that way, but she'll also make sure you know what it's really for. It's for clock golf and boules; for pell mell and pot green. It's for turning into an outdoor theatre and coping with tents and slides and swings.

Your garden may not win any prizes in local competitions, but as far as your family is concerned it'll be the tops if it's a place for fun and games, rather than for double digging and earnest composting.

I reckon you *can* have a garden *and* enjoy it, and this book proves that point to a nicety.

PLANNING A LAWN

Why have a lawn?

'Nothing is more pleasant to the eye than green grass finely shorn.' So said the essayist Francis Bacon, in praise of what for centuries since has been the envy of gardeners across the world, the great British lawn. Just imagine, then, how many people must have been turning in their graves over more recent years as so many million square yards of turf have been ripped up and replaced by the ubiquitous paving slab! But this wide scale destruction of our greatest asset has gone on long enough. It's time to call a halt. So, exit concrete, enter the lawn.

There really is no justification for a garden of wall-to-wall paving. Ease of maintenance is the most commonly proffered excuse but, as anyone with even the smallest patio will know, hard landscaping demands constant cleaning and sweeping in order to keep it looking spick and span. The work involved in maintaining a lawn is no greater and, let's face it, if you can brandish a broom, you can manage a mower. Of one thing you can be absolutely certain, your efforts will be far better rewarded. And, more important still, those rewards will come year in, year out.

From here on, grass scores points over paving every time. So much so that the latter no longer even warrants a mention. The green of a lawn is relaxing and pleasing to the eye, acting as a perfect foil to all the plants and special features you wish to include in the garden. The grass feels good to the touch, especially underfoot, and is soft and forgiving. The turf is a luxurious carpet, tailored to fit what, in effect, is an outdoor room – a place to play, to entertain or simply to relax. In essence, an expanse of lawn just begs to be used.

Sadly, that most off-putting of signs, 'keep off the grass', has instilled in many the idea that grass can be looked at but not touched. The truth is that there are basically two types of lawn – one purely ornamental, made up of the finer types of grass, and the other utility, using coarser varieties that will stand up to wear and tear. Choose a suitable mixture and you can look forward to having a lawn that will take any amount of punishment and look good into the bargain.

So how you intend to use your lawn is just one of the factors that has to be considered at the planning stage. Another is the aspect of your plot – which part gets the most sun, for example – so that you can shape your lawn and position special features to advantage. There's no great secret to creating a lawn that will give lasting pleasure. And it certainly doesn't require any degree of skill. All you have to do is give it the very best start in life and, as you will see, it will be your most rewarding downpayment yet on a long-term investment!

Lawn Statistics

According to the *Gardening 1987 Mintel Special Report*, out of the 20.8 million households in the UK, there are 18.2 million with gardens, 15.2 million of which include a lawn. Somewhat perplexing, however, is the fact that only 13.6 million own a mower! Approximately one-third (31 percent) of all lawns measure up to 38sq yd, while 20 percent are 38–75sq yd, 24 percent are 75–150sq yd, 15 percent are 150–300 sq yd, 17 percent are 300–600sq yd and 3 percent over 600sq yd. The average lawn is calculated as measuring 111–138sq yd and, perhaps rather surprisingly, is said to take up only 25–50 percent of the entire garden. Incidentally, 7 percent of garden owners, when asked the size of their lawn, didn't have a clue!

When you destroy a blade of grass
You poison England at her roots
GORDON BOTTOMLEY (1874–1948)

Two lawns (opposite) with quite different characteristics yet both just begging to be used for relaxation and entertainment. The broad expanse of lawn (top) is ideal for family games and yet a seat in a shady corner allows for quiet contemplation – the perfect 'growing-up lawn'. The bold curves and pool in the lawn below provide a charming setting for sitting, sunbathing and eating al fresco but still leave enough space for more active pursuits – a fine example of the 'maturing lawn'

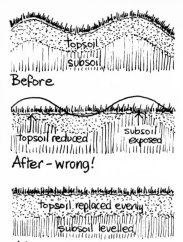

Good ground preparation and a level site is vital when starting a lawn from scratch. Be sure to maintain an adequate and even layer of fertile topsoil

Ten Tips for Lawn Renovation

1. Assess the site, identifying weeds and other troubles. If the lawn grass is basically healthy and plentiful, it's worthwhile renovating it rather than starting from scratch.
2. Ideally in spring but otherwise in autumn, cut down all vegetation to a manageable height – about 2in above ground level. It may be a good idea to hire a rotary mower to do the job.
3. Rake off the cuttings and you will now be able to see quite clearly the problems that need to be tackled.
4. Mow the lawn at a high setting, reducing the cut over a number of weeks to the desired level.
5. Use a selective weedkiller to kill weeds and moss.
6. Get rid of as much dead grass (thatch) and unwanted debris as possible, using a rake and stiff brush.
7. Attend to bumps and hollows in the lawn by cutting an 'H' shape in the turf over the problem area. Carefully slide a spade beneath the turf, working from the centre of the 'H', and then fold back the flaps on either side. Excess soil can now be removed or added as necessary before replacing the turf.
8. Aerate the lawn and apply a top-dressing.
9. At least six weeks after using the weedkiller, re-seed any bare patches, ideally having applied a spring or autumn fertiliser about one week beforehand.
10. Tidy up edges and continue to treat any weeds or diseases.

Making a start

If you're lucky, you've maybe moved into a new house where the garden is simply a bare plot. Or you might have inherited a veritable jungle that will need to be completely cleared. You may even have had to strip the whole site of those unmentionable concrete flags. In each case, you have a decided advantage because you will be starting from scratch and, very often, that is the only way to achieve a lawn that will serve you well and do justice to your garden.

A bare plot is like an empty canvas in that it allows you to build a garden in the same way as an artist would paint a picture. Free of any constraints in terms of existing features, you can use your creativity to add shape, colour and texture to form a totally original and personal image.

But what use is a masterpiece if it peels and flakes? Just as the quality and tone of the paint relies on that canvas being well primed, so a successful lawn depends on good ground preparation. And that is why even those who have an existing lawn might be better off starting afresh if it is in a particularly bad state of repair. A certain amount of renovation work is feasible, of course – a few weeds can be eradicated, bald patches resown, the odd bump levelled, edges reshaped – but anything more than that is likely to prove a waste of effort.

The lie of the land

Assuming, for now, that you are starting a lawn from scratch, the first thing to do is assess the state of the ground. The type of soil in your garden will largely dictate your choice of grass mixture. If it's moist and heavy it will be better suited to coarser species, while a light, free-draining soil is perfect for fine, ornamental varieties. However, much can be done to improve the nature of your soil – by incorporating organic matter if it is sandy, chalky or stony, or by improving drainage with the addition of coarse sand if it is heavy loam, peaty or clay – and this will pay dividends later on. A medium loam is the ideal.

But it is the topsoil that is particularly important because, unlike the subsoil, it contains varying degrees of humus and so affects fertility. It is this top layer – which, ideally, should be at least 6in deep – that provides the necessary nutrients to make your grass grow healthily. Apart from the improvements mentioned above, peaty soils will benefit from the addition of lime, while a good, balanced fertiliser will make sandy soils more fertile. If you don't have sufficient topsoil, or if it is particularly poor and needs replacing, you will have to buy some in from a local supplier.

Maintaining a sufficient and even depth of topsoil is something you must take into account if any levelling of the site is necessary. And if you are to make the most of your lawn, of course, the flatter it is the better. A slope may be easy enough to mow, and it can also look very attractive, but it won't do you any favours when it comes to playing games or positioning furniture and barbecues, etc. So, even if you have only a slightly sloping plot, you will have to set about accurately levelling it. If the angle is severe you will probably have to incorporate terraces.

In both cases, to do this properly will require a considerable

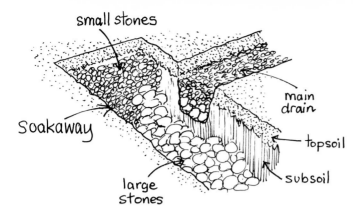

small stones

main drain

Soakaway

topsoil

large stones

subsoil

If the garden, or one particular area, is heavily waterlogged, it will be necessary to incorporate a drainage system. This involves creating a soakaway – usually at the lowest point – which is fed by a herringbone network of channels. Seek expert advice before embarking on any major work of this kind

amount of earth moving, and so in order to preserve the topsoil, it will first have to be completely removed – do one side of the plot first – while you level the subsoil underneath. This can be done by driving pegs into the ground at regular intervals and checking that they are at a uniform height by resting a spirit level and a plank of wood over their tops. Then it's a relatively simple matter to move the earth around until it is level with the pegs.

All that remains is for the ground to be trodden down, double checked for accuracy and, if all is well, the topsoil replaced in an even layer over the levelled surface. Now is the time to dig over the whole area, to the depth of a spade. If the thought of that is too much to bear, consider hiring a mechanical cultivator to do the job. Be careful not to dig too deeply, though – the last thing you want to do is disturb the subsoil and bring that up to the surface.

Initial ground preparation is the same whether you intend to create a lawn from seed or turf. And we'll be coming to the pros and cons of each later on. Right now, though, there's a far more crucial decision to be made – namely, what shape should your lawn be? The time is right to make a garden plan . . .

Drawing a plan

It's nigh on impossible to visualise how you would like your garden to look when you are standing in its midst – especially if it is no more than a sea of earth. What you want is a bird's eye view of the plot so that you can assess its shape and the position of any existing features in one fell swoop. A scaled plan of your garden will prove indispensable in this respect, allowing you to mark down essential detail and experiment with alternative ideas to your heart's content. Then, when you've come up with the plan you think is best on paper, you can safely set about making your dream a reality. (See an example on page 92.)

Another important reason for making a plan is that it will help you to decide where to position special features – like, say, a barbecue unit or adventure play area – to best advantage. You can pinpoint the spots that get the most sun or shade and the areas that are most sheltered or exposed. If necessary, you can plan to provide additional shelter from wind or from the heat of the midday sun. You can also identify any areas that have difficult soil conditions, are heavily shaded or are likely to suffer from the most wear and tear, so that you can choose a suitable grass mixture for

Soil Testing

Soil testing will determine the degree of acidity or alkalinity in your soil and, in turn, will help you choose an appropriate soil improver and suitable grass mixture. Do-it-yourself soil test kits are readily available and will prove enormously beneficial, not only in establishing a lawn but in choosing plants for particular areas of your garden. Acidity is measured as a pH and the ideal level is between 5.5 and 6.5, which is only slightly acid. The lower the pH, the higher the acidity. To correct excessive acidity, you add lime or chalk. To increase acidity on alkaline soils (that is, lower the pH), you incorporate moss peat and sulphur. Soil test kits and meters are simple to use and are reasonably priced at under £10.

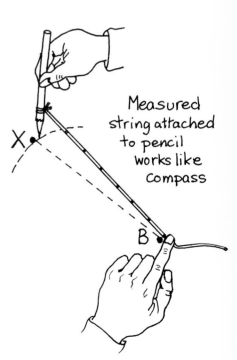

Measured string attached to pencil works like compass

X

B

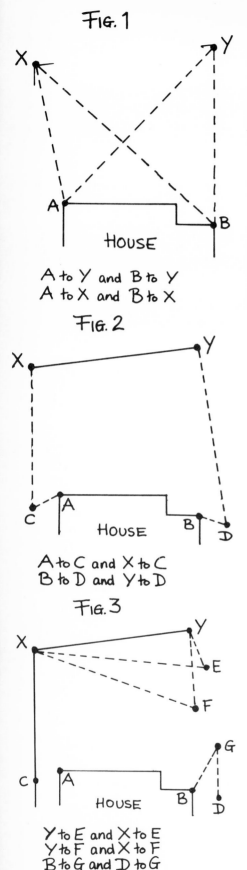

FIG. 1

A to Y and B to Y
A to X and B to X

FIG. 2

A to C and X to C
B to D and Y to D

FIG. 3

Y to E and X to E
Y to F and X to F
B to G and D to G

them. Bear in mind, too, that any major construction work, like the creation of permanent seating units, barbecues or garden pools, is best carried out prior to laying the lawn so as to avoid badly damaging the turf.

All of the above will to some extent influence the shape of your lawn. So, too, will the way in which you intend to use the available space. The success of your final design will depend on how effectively you can combine both the practical and aesthetic considerations. And from that point of view, those with existing lawns will find drawing a plan equally useful, as they will be able to see far more easily how the garden could be improved or better tailored to their needs.

Measuring up

Even the most simple, rectangular plot is unlikely to be quite as straight-sided and symmetrical as it appears. Of course a regular shape like this will be far easier to transfer onto a plan than one that meanders and turns this way and that, but in both cases the basic technique of measuring and plotting is the same.

You'll need to arm yourself with a reel of twine or string, a number of lengths of cane or pieces of stick to act as pegs, a measuring tape or rod, and a notepad and pencil. If possible, get someone to help you. Then simply proceed as follows, making the necessary sketches and noting down measurements as you go along:

★ Take the back of the house (or that part of it that faces the garden) as your starting point. Measure the width and make a note of any protrusions or recesses.

★ Take two points on the house – preferably the corners or as far apart as possible – and mark these as your 'fixed' markers (A and B). Then, using the twine and pegs, measure from each fixed point to the top corners (X and Y) of your garden (*Fig 1*). This will determine the angle and position of your top boundary.

★ To plot the angle and position of the side boundaries (*Fig 2*), first choose a spot on each side that is close to the house (C and D). Now measure, in turn, to each of these from your fixed points (A and B respectively) and from your corner points (X and Y respectively).

★ If your side or top boundaries are irregular, you can plot their shape accurately by inserting pegs along their length at measured intervals (E, F and G) and measuring the distance from each of these to one of your fixed points (*Fig 3*). Just like dot-to-dot drawings, the more points you have, the more effective the result will be.

★ Finally, if you have any existing features, like a tree or shed, pinpoint these using the same principal (*Fig 4*). Remember to mark not only the position of the trunk of a tree but also the area of the canopy – measure from around the trunk, using string and pegs, to do this accurately.

★ Where the plot is particularly irregular – L-shaped, for example – it will be necessary to sub-divide the area into manageable sections. Measure the one nearest to the house first and then progress to the next, using the fixed points you have already established to plot others as necessary (*Fig 5*).

10

On to paper

The best idea is to use graph paper with tracing paper over the top. That way, any mistakes can be easily altered and, when it comes to filling in detail, you can start again from scratch if necessary without having to redraw the 'master' plan. The scale you choose will depend on the size of the garden but it will be limited to some extent by the paper – you don't want it to fill the living room yet it must be large enough to allow for accurate representation of features. As a rule of thumb, a scale of 1:50 should suffice – in other words, say, 1in representing 4ft. And once you have plotted the master, of course, you can always increase the scale of individual sections to add more detail.

You translate your measurements on to paper by, in effect, retracing your steps. Instead of using string and pegs, you use a compass to represent the measurements between the various points. For example, in relation to *Fig 1* you would first adjust the compass, according to your scale, to represent the measurements A to X and B to X. Then, having already marked the points A and B on the graph paper, of course, you fix the point of the compass on each in turn and create an arc at the measured point. Where the arcs cross becomes point X, and so forth.

Once all the points are marked in this way you can join them up and mark in any existing features. This is now your 'master', so don't make any further marks on it. Instead, use sheets of tracing paper over the top – by the score if necessary – to start playing around with lawn shapes and creating special features!

Shaping a lawn

First and foremost there are a few basic design principles that will help you achieve a visually pleasing lawn, whatever its size and however you are going to be using it. And if you bear these in mind when it comes to accommodating the practicalities, you'll be able to reach a far more effective compromise. Most lawns, for example, benefit from having as large an area as possible left uncluttered, free of any permanent obstructions. And most look better for having outlines that make a positive statement, be they sweeping curves or straight lines. Generally, a lawn should act as a unifying backcloth to the garden as a whole, reflecting its character – formal or informal, say – and enhancing its plantings and special features.

In a formal garden (*Fig A*) the lawn can be a precision built rectangle with maybe the addition of a simple diagonal to slightly offset the symmetry. Here you have the easiest lawn to maintain and the fullest scope for the positioning of features around the edges and in the corners. The design also makes maximum use of the space available and is therefore particularly well suited to smaller gardens where the lawn is to be used for playing ball games and so forth.

In larger gardens and those smaller ones that are to be used mainly for relaxation and entertainment you can afford to be slightly more daring. A meandering, informal lawn shape (*Fig B*) still retains a fairly open central area yet provides intrigue and invites exploration because the whole garden can't be seen at once. It will also make smaller gardens appear larger. Here the

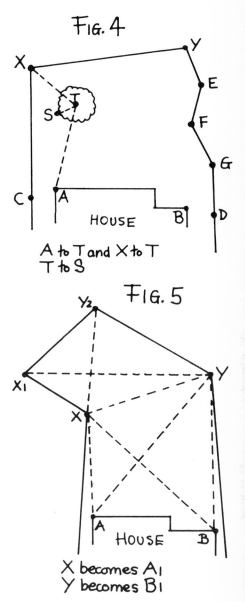

FIG. 4

A to T and X to T
T to S

FIG. 5

X becomes A1
Y becomes B1

Terracing Tip

If your lawn is to be terraced, plan to include plants at the base of any retaining walls. First, they will soften what could otherwise be an overly harsh horizontal line. Second, the border in which you plant them can be edged with bricks or stones that are sunk below the level of the lawn in order to make mowing that much easier (see 'Structures and Special Features'). Where there are several terraces within the lawn, aim to link them visually by using the same materials and plants.

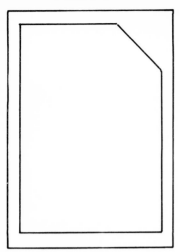

FIG. A

Formal...

FIG. B

Informal...

FIG. C

Fun!

recesses become natural homes for garden furniture, etc, the projecting curves an ideal setting for focal points. And there's also plenty of opportunity to create secret hideaways.

Taking the same principle even further, it is possible to create quite complex lawn shapes that, in effect, provide you with a series of outdoor rooms (*Fig C*). Here, each area can be treated quite differently and you can incorporate all manner of features within your garden without them all fighting for attention. Even in a relatively small garden, it could be an ideal arrangement if sitting, sunbathing and eating alfresco are your main priorities. It would be important to maintain a main 'aisle' of lawn, however, otherwise you might end up with a maze, and you would have to choose any screens or 'dividers' very carefully to avoid the cell-block syndrome.

When planning a sweeping, informal lawn, always make the curves bold and expansive. There's nothing worse than a half-hearted wavy edge and, at the other extreme, anything too frilly will make mowing a real chore. Similarly, if you are going for straight lines, make sure they are! Angles are more difficult to incorporate successfully and you should make sure they are serving a definite purpose before getting too carried away. Again, though, be positive and make them as bold as possible.

Special requirements
You'll be lucky indeed if you are in a position to view your lawn on purely aesthetic grounds. More likely than not you will need to consider the day-to-day running of your garden as well, which might mean incorporating into your garden plan a shed, green-house, service path, vegetable patch and utility area. The only real solution here is to simply cut your losses in terms of the space available to you for a lawn.

Rather than try to accommodate such items within the lawn, which will never be particularly satisfactory, make provision for them at the outset, aiming to keep them to the perimeter of your plot wherever possible. Then, by using ornamental screens to hide them from view, you can have an uninterrupted, albeit smaller, expanse of land on which to create the lawn of your dreams.

The ultimate shape of your lawn might also be affected by the need to avoid, say, an area of especially dense shade or of badly waterlogged ground – that is, if you can't do anything to rectify the situation. This illustrates, yet again, the importance of properly assessing your site and marking all the relevant details on your plan. If you are aware of the problems, after all, you're already halfway to solving them.

And the more accurate and detailed your plan, of course, the better equipped you will be to incorporate all the special features and fun ideas detailed within this book. Don't worry about creating the lawn yet – first find out how you can make the very best use of it.

THE GROWING-UP LAWN

'Go and play in the garden' is the all too familiar and desperate cry when youngsters are getting under your feet and your house appears to be getting smaller by the minute. The floors are probably strewn with discarded playthings, the cupboards packed with long forgotten toys and games. Nothing will please them, but nothing would please you more than some peace and quiet!

It's hardly surprising, then, that being sent outside to play is frequently regarded by children as some sort of custodial sentence rather than the treat it should be. The reprieve, when they're called in for lunch or tea, just can't come soon enough.

And invariably the garden itself is equally to blame – an empty expanse of lawn relieved, at best, by a token tree or two and a few unfriendly flowerbeds. All you need is some railings and you've got a penitentiary. You certainly haven't got a playground!

While it is generally accepted that children need to be kept amused indoors, there's a strange theory that they can be left to their own devices as soon as they are exposed to the elements and are supposedly communing with nature. The home houses every conceivable form of entertainment, from magic crayons to computer games, but the garden, in effect, is an empty room.

Admittedly all children are masters in the art of make-believe, but even here a nudge in the right direction wouldn't go amiss. At the very least, you ought to create an environment that will fire their imagination – with lots of secret hideaways, for example – and you ought to be willing to provide an endless supply of basic and interesting props.

The nature of these will depend on the age of the children, of course, but they needn't be expensive or sophisticated – it could be anything from an old tablecloth or tarpaulin to a collection of plastic flower pots or a couple of buckets. Tiny tots are especially easy to please in this respect. After all, isn't that cardboard box always far more fun than the expensive toy inside?

As children grow and become less inclined to muse away the hours playing pretend, they also become more demanding and materialistic. They want real things, which cost money. The trouble here, though, is that they still have that rather tiresome trait of not wanting anything that is handed to them on a plate. You could turn your lawn into a miniature Alton Towers, crammed with brand new fancy swings, slides, climbing frames and see-saws to the exclusion of all else, but it wouldn't impress them for long. It might be a real hit initially – and your children would certainly discover an awful lot of new friends – but all too soon the novelty would wear off. They'll outgrow it before you've even finished paying for it!

Rather than putting all your eggs in one basket, it is far better

Plants to Avoid
No matter how safe you think the plants in your garden are – and only a tiny minority of all plants are dangerous – it's a good idea to teach children not to eat the leaves, fruits, seeds or flowers of any growing plant. The following is a list of the more common plants that are part or wholly poisonous and will cause illness if consumed:
- Yew ● Aquilegia ● Buttercup
- Common Spindle Tree ● Daphne mezereum ● Delphinium
- Euphorbia ● Foxglove ● Heaths and heathers● Ivy ● Laburnum ● Lily
- Lupin● Monkshood (Aconitum)
- Privet● Robinia ● Viburnum
- Yucca

Invest in just one item of play equipment like this super four-in-one swing and you can dispense with squabbles and keep children of all ages amused for hours

to make provision for a whole range of different activities, from make-believe and creative play to organised games, sport and recreation. That way, the children have a much wider choice of things to amuse them and you have a much better chance of finding play ideas and features that will meet the constraints of both your garden and your bank balance.

There are your own constraints as well, of course, and you don't want to go so far as to make the garden a no-go zone for adults! With a little imagination, you can create a garden that will keep the whole family amused, from toddlers and teenagers to grown-ups and grannies. And the secret here is to opt for relatively simple and inexpensive features that can be easily dismantled or modified in some way to perform a different role as the children mature. A sandpit could be transformed into a garden pool, for example, or a climbing frame could be turned into a pergola, laden with scented climbers. Planning ahead is the key.

Allowing for spontaneity is another good reason for not providing an instant playground. If you watch your children at play you will see what amuses them most and you can respond more or less on demand – within reason! This way, playthings or games can be devised to suit not only their personality but their rate of development as well.

14

This approach requires a certain amount of involvement on your part, of course, which raises the question of supervision. In theory, a garden holds far fewer potential dangers than the average household. And, in turn, it is relatively easy to make your garden a safe environment for children. How great a priority you make this will determine the degree to which you can leave your offspring to their own devices.

You can't get a more forgiving surface than a lawn when it comes to falls or rough and tumble. So it makes sense to keep hard areas to a minimum and well away from the play area – preferably even cordoned off. If your garden isn't level, any drops should be shielded by, say, a wall high enough not to be climbed, a trellis screen or a thick ornamental hedge. Certainly make sure any accidental 'landings' will at least be soft ones!

Anything portable in a garden is a potential hazard and that includes tools and machinery of course. Always keep these items firmly behind lock and key. Other less obvious danger areas are garden ornaments or statues that could be knocked over, furniture that can be folded up or toppled, and fencing and railings with spaces that could trap little heads. Also, sunken garden pools, however shallow, are out of the question when you have little children as they could so easily trip up and fall in. Safe alternatives are bubble fountains and water funnels, both of which make superb features and will be appreciated by kids and adults alike. All it takes to play safe is a little thought!

For complete peace of mind it's also important to consider the plants in your garden. OK, so we don't want to get carried away and just as toddlers soon discover that fire means hot, so will children quickly learn that holly means prickles. Nevertheless, it would be a good idea to place any of your more noxious or vulnerable plants out of harm's way and to restrict plantings in the

Give the children a place of their own and they'll love you for it. Make it as sophisticated as this house on stilts and you'll also have a charming and original focal point

15

A novel and attractive solution to your storage problems – downstairs this robust building from Barrel-Play Ltd is a mini-shed, upstairs it's a playhouse for the kids

play area to innocuous toughies. Remember, too, that a few quite common garden plants are poisonous – to a lesser or greater extent, in whole or in part – and obviously you will want to avoid these if you have very young children.

However safe the garden is, you'll still want to have under-fives playing close to the house, at least within ear-shot. Ideally you should be able to keep an eye on them from, say, the kitchen or living room window, which is something to bear in mind when it comes to siting playthings or laying your lawn if you're starting from scratch. Older children will relish the idea of being as far away from you as possible and that's when it's a good idea to start creating secret corners or screened off areas within your lawn – and as much for your benefit as theirs! After all, an adventure playground is hardly a visual delight.

Turning your garden over to the kids certainly doesn't mean you have to give up on it. But as there's more than a little of the child in the best of us, if you find you're fighting a losing battle, you might as well surrender and join in the fun.

A place of their own

With constant reminders of what they can or can't have and where they can or can't go, it's hardly surprising that children develop an awareness of property and territory at such an early age. And it's because the word can't is so much more familiar, of course, that they are so appreciative of a special gift or a place they can call their own – like a Wendy house, for example.

Somewhere on the lawn for toddlers to sit, eat, play and entertain is likely to prove just as popular. And by setting aside a specific area for the purpose, and making it a permanent feature, the effect will be far more convincing than if you were to simply cart out a table and a few chairs from the house.

First of all, choose a sheltered, cosy site – maybe even screened on two or three sides – to give the children a sense of privacy and to create the impression of an outdoor room. Then you simply have to build some small-scale garden furniture that will meet the demands of little people at play.

Paving stones set on top of brick plinths work well, or you could use smooth timber planks atop concrete blocks. Rather more rustic – and a lot of fun – would be sawn logs, a large one being used as the table and smaller ones making the seats. And if you think the surfaces might be a bit cold or rough for sitting on, simply keep a few old cushions to hand.

One of the simplest ways to create mini tables and seats for toddlers is to use sawn logs – be sure to smooth down the bare wood and coat with varnish to avoid splinters

If you're not a DIY buff, you could buy a scaled-down timber picnic table, which has integral bench seats. Specially designed for children, these are now widely available – along with the full-grown versions – and are very reasonably priced. Usually they come untreated, which gives you the opportunity to add an attractive coloured preservative or woodstain.

If the furniture is permanent it will be impossible to mow the grass in the small spaces in between. So to save fiddly cutting by hand, the area immediately underneath could be replaced with decorative pebbles, sand or ornamental bark. And a final thought – if you're having a garden party, the tables and seats can be pressed into action for laying out food, bottles and glasses.

log seat and table

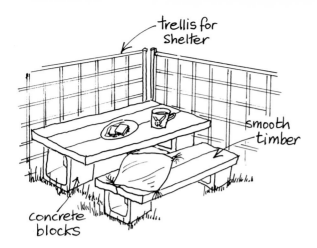

trellis for shelter

smooth timber

concrete blocks

Making a sandpit

Playing with sand provides endless fascination and fun for the under-fives, including the tiniest of tots who have yet to find their feet. Of course, you could improvise by using, say, a washing-up bowl as a container but it is hardly likely to set their imagination on fire. Far more irresistible would be a good-sized, permanent pit that can also be designed to make an attractive feature within the lawn.

Another good reason for taking special care over design and construction is that at a later date, when you consider it safe, you can transform the pit into a garden pool. After all, the same basic principles are involved in both and the ideal dimensions for a pool are also perfect for a sandpit.

First of all, then, you want to choose the best site. A sandpit will need to be as close to the house as possible – probably almost on the lawn's edge and maybe adjacent to a patio. If you have a path through the lawn it would make sense to site the pit alongside that. Thinking ahead, bear in mind that a pool should be well clear of overhanging trees and should receive plenty of sunlight, which is no bad idea for a sandpit either (you can always use a parasol to provide shade in the height of summer). Finally, the ground must be perfectly level.

By far the easiest and quickest way to create a sandpit is to buy a pre-formed pool from a garden centre or specialist water garden supplier. These are made from heavy-duty plastic and come in all sorts of imaginative shapes, some even with realistic rock-like formations. Most important for our purposes, though, is the fact that they are usually constructed to provide at least one change in level – at their simplest, a deeper central well surrounded by a slightly higher ledge. Understandably, the reason behind this has a lot more to do with water gardening than sandpit making, but for us it is ideal because the sand can be confined to the deepest section and the 'shelf' can be used by the children as seating or as a play surface.

A pool like this can be dropped into an excavation of roughly the same shape and back-filled with earth around the sides to keep it stable. Just make sure the base is properly supported, preferably on a layer of sand, and that it is level. Also, that the rim of the pool, or sandpit, is slightly below the level of the lawn to allow for the use of an edging stone or, alternatively, to make mowing up to the edges that much easier.

There's really no limit as far as size is concerned, although the ideal overall depth is about 18in. It would be as well to go for the largest you can reasonably fit into the allocated site, if only because when it comes to the pool conversion you will regret being landed with little more than a bathtub. Certainly, from the children's point of view, the bigger the sandpit, the better they can make it a world of their own.

Having a ledge around the pit also makes it far easier to sweep back any scattered or spilt sand, and so it's worthwhile incorporating a similar device if you are going to design and build a sandpit from scratch. The simplest way to do this is to excavate a rectangle, say 6ft by 4ft by 9in, and then make a further, central hole, this time of 4ft by 2ft by 9in. A lining of concrete is all that is needed for now (when it becomes a pond you'll have to apply a waterproof sealant) and you may like to finish off the ledge with some smooth, round-edged coping stones – just to make it more comfortable and aesthetically pleasing.

It's no good having sand without water, of course, and so you should also try to ensure there's a fairly plentiful supply somewhere close by. For real tiny tots, a small bucket or watering can would probably suffice. For toddlers and older children, though, a novel solution might be an old-fashioned waterpump (you can get all sorts of decorative, reproduction ones these days) so that they can fill containers themselves, as and when they please. It would make a great focal point in the garden and, unlike a garden tap, you wouldn't be running to turn it off all the time.

Playthings for toddlers, including a sandpit, should be sited close to the house, preferably within view but at least within earshot

Before

After

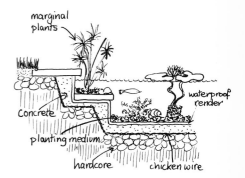

marginal plants

Concrete

waterproof render

planting medium

hardcore   chicken wire

Turn a Pit into a Pool

Once the children have outgrown the sandpit it can be converted into a garden pool. And the better it is constructed, the easier it will be. Once the pit is emptied of sand the inner surface will have to be waterproofed, if it isn't already. This can be done by applying a waterproof concrete render to the entire surface, followed by a coat of proprietary sealant, or by inserting a polythene liner, the edges of which would have to be anchored and buried beneath an edging stone.

The pool can then be filled with water, ready for stocking with plants, fish and snails to create a well-balanced underwater environment. The number of plants and fish you can include will depend on the surface area of the pool. A depth of 18in is vital, however, for all deep-water aquatics and also goldfish, while marginal plants will need to be stood no deeper than about 9in.

Plants can be grown in special aquatic baskets, which simply rest on the floor or shelf of the pool, or in a layer of compost covered with gravel. The best planting time is between April and early August. There are floating plants, too, which are simply left on the surface, and there are the all-important oxygenators, which are completely submerged and prevent the water turning green and slimy.

Wait a couple of weeks before adding any fish. But, remember, if you fancy the idea of encouraging frogs to take up residence and breed, leave the fish out altogether, or they'll eat the tadpoles.

One rather unfortunate aspect of a sandpit is that it's likely to prove as irresistible to the neighbourhood cats as it is to the children. To play safe, a good idea is to provide some sort of cover for the pit when it is not in use. A piece of plastic sheeting would suffice but, apart from it looking decidedly unattractive, it would tend to collect pools of rainwater and so become quite unmanageable. A much better idea would be to stretch some netting over a wood frame, or to find a panel of plastic or timber trellis that could be cut to the appropriate shape.

So, give children a sandpit, some water and a few basic implements and they'll need little encouragement or help from you to while away the hours. In fact, before long, all manner of secret worlds with strange inhabitants will be shaped from the sand and, more likely than not, the only sandcastles in evidence will be the ones you've built yourself!

Playing house

A Wendy house of some description is a must as toddlers will quickly make it their own private place, where they can feel secure, cosy and content. After all, when you are knee high to a garden gnome, the great outdoors is likely to seem more than a little menacing.

That's why it is also important to get the scale of the playhouse just right – too big and it will be austere and uninviting, too small and it will be impractical and unconvincing. Ideally, it should be able to house up to four little ones in comfort, so that they can stand up, sit down and have enough space left for a few playthings. Certainly don't try to make one playhouse or camp do for both toddlers and older children as their requirements are quite different (see 'Climbing frames').

Versatile kit-form structures (top left) are available from Hillian Interlog. The same basic design can be used first for a sandpit and later for a raised island bed or even a garden pool

Little children will be perfectly happy with a relatively simple, lightweight structure and many of the ones available from large stores and toy departments are perfectly adequate. Some of these are really sophisticated, in fact, with charming details, imaginative colour schemes and windows that open, etc. They are usually made from some sort of heavy duty plastic, which is stretched over a wood or metal frame, and they often have an integral floor – important if the ground is damp.

The great advantage of all shop-bought playhouses is that they are extremely safe, are light enough to move around the garden at will – to save wear and tear of your lawn – and can be quickly dismantled and packed away for storage whenever necessary. They'll soon deteriorate if left out in all weathers.

These are points worth bearing in mind if you're into DIY and fancy building a playhouse yourself. And if you do, of course, you can let your imagination run riot and create something totally original. Just remember to pay attention to safety – for example, no splintery wood, no exposed nails, no toxic paints or preservatives, no danger of collapse – and you can test your carpentry skills to the limit.

An all-wood playhouse will be extremely heavy and cumbersome and, as such, would be far better suited to older children – probably as a permanent feature for adventure play. For toddlers the key is to devise a means of reducing the weight and making the structure portable.

One way would be to make timber frames that can be clad with panels of hardboard and then hinged together – just like a folding screen. The ends would then be fitted with bolts to keep the structure rigid. You really want a minimum of three panels – in which case you'd have a tent shape with a floor – but you could use four or six to make a proper cube shape. An easy way of creating a detachable roof and floor would be to use plastic or canvas panels, which could be laced to the framework by means of metal eyelets. Indeed, the whole structure could be made in this way if you preferred.

The advantage of hardboard is that you can cut out any number of doors and windows and the panels will remain rigid. You can also create fun shapes along the top projecting edges to form, say, turrets, battlements or chimneys. But the playhouse doesn't have to be reminiscent of a building: it could be a spaceship or a boat, or even a favourite children's character – the only restriction is your imagination and your talent with a paintbrush. Hopefully, you'll have as much fun making the playhouse as the children will have playing in it!

Slides

Slides are best shop bought as they will be safer, more effective and practical than anything you can make at home. And as long as the children can climb safely up to the top of the chute, they can be as tall or twisty, long or lumpy, as money allows. The kids will love them, whether they shoot down head-first or feet-first, on their tummies or on their bottoms!

For toddlers it is particularly important that the climb to the top shouldn't be too arduous, otherwise they'll get frustrated and you'll

20

end up becoming the human lift. Also, the steps and top 'landing' should be enclosed to prevent a fall – although this isn't so imperative on very small slides – and the chute should be deep enough to stop little ones whizzing over the edge.

By siting the slide on the lawn – well clear of any hard surfaces or obstacles – you will be minimising the consequences of a possible tumble. However, you will soon find that the surrounding area, and especially the patch of lawn at the end of the slide, is taking more than its fair share of punishment.

If the slide is too heavy to move around – to give the lawn a chance to recover – then it might be worthwhile setting it in a specially created pit filled with shredded bark. This could be made to look extremely attractive, especially if you make it into a pleasing shape and define it with an edging material of some description – cobbles or logs, for example. Alternatively, you could sow the area with an extra tough variety of grass seed.

In the swing

For babies and toddlers, being sat in a swing without someone there to push would be about as much fun as being put in the stocks! Active involvement on your part is essential, as is responsible supervision – even with a totally enclosed swing, it would be unwise to leave little ones to the mercy of a slightly older brother or sister. It might not be inherently dangerous but it could prove upsetting if the pusher was to get over zealous.

Swings for children of this age, then, are demanding on your time and of relatively short-term interest. So if your lawn is quite small, a standard swing on a frame – which takes up a fair amount of space and needs a permanent site – might not be a particularly good investment at this stage. It would be more justifiable if you have older children as well, of course, but remember that toddlers really ought to have an enclosed seat and that's unlikely to appeal to a six-year-old's sense of fun!

An alternative would be one of the mini-swings that are sold by good toy shops these days, which are designed especially for smaller children and have a frame that can be dismantled for storage. They're perfectly stable yet they're so compact they can even be used indoors.

If you have a robust branch overhanging your lawn, all your problems are solved. You can hang a home-made swing from this and it will cost you next to nothing. In the absence of a suitable tree, you could build an attractive timber archway – to span a path, say, or to visually frame a focal point – and suspend a swing from that. By fitting hooks to the ropes or chains and eyes to the crossbeam, the swing can then be hung up or removed in a matter of seconds.

One way of creating the swing itself is from a child's old wooden highchair with the legs sawn off – if you haven't got one to hand you could try scouring a few junk shops. Alternatively, you can construct an armchair-type seat yourself using lengths of timber for the main framework, plywood for the seat and dowel-rods for the uprights in between. In both cases, the easiest way of securing the child is to use an old belt – simply strap it across the front, between the uprights on either side.

Taking the Strain

Where patches of grass are going to be handed out severe punishment on a regular basis – for example, where the pusher stands behind a swing or at the end of a slide – it might be necessary to take additional precautions to save wear and tear. Replacing the at-risk turf with shredded bark has been suggested as one effective solution to the problem but, ideally, a far better idea would be to re-seed the area with a grass that will take any amount of trampling and scuffing. Two such lawn seeds, in domestic-sized packs, are Elka and Hunter, both of which use dwarf fine-leaved rye grasses developed specifically for amenity use. In fact, Elka is supplied to Wembley Stadium!

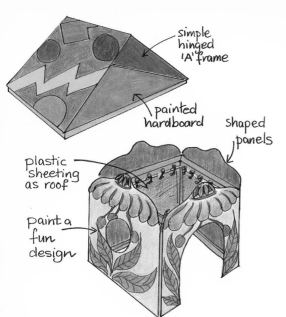

simple
hinged
'A' frame

painted
hardboard

shaped
panels

plastic
sheeting
as roof

paint a
fun
design

While toddlers will be happy with simple, lightweight playhouses (left), older children will want something more robust. The log climbing frame (above) doesn't require any great carpentry skills and the basic structure can also be used to form an exciting camp-cum-slide (top right)

If do-it-yourself doesn't appeal you can buy ready-made structures that have maximum play appeal and look terrific into the bargain

Slides are best bought from specialist manufacturers, even if they are to be incorporated into a DIY structure, as above. The one shown here is being used with a water-splashing Slippy Slide

Toddlers will love this mini-swing in its very own little house. And, what's more, it's light enough to be moved around at will

Tricycle track

Push and pull trucks, pedal cars, tricycles – the lawn will be the automatic destination for anything, or anybody, on wheels. Think how much more fun it would be, though, to have a special track, where the children can steer a course, count their laps and even race against their friends.

A figure of eight will give the greatest length of track without taking up too much space, and it will also be a lot more exciting than a simple circle or oval. To help you get the shape right when it comes to excavation – you'll need a shallow trench to take the paving stones – you can arrange a garden hosepipe or washing line on the lawn and use this as a template.

Sink the paving into a bed of sand to give stability and leave a slight gap between the slabs to soften the effect. The spaces and edges can then be sown with a tough grass mixture – adding more topsoil where necessary – or they can be topped up with more sand. If the area isn't going to be sown, use an edging material to protect the lawn and contain the sand.

For the sake of a few extra paving stones, it would be worthwhile incorporating a turning point at the centre, while to finish off you could plant the two inner areas with some tough, spongy shrubs, dwarf conifers and ground cover plants. Then you've also got a really striking island bed!

Climbing frames

Unless you are a welder by trade, metal climbing frames are best bought from specialist play equipment manufacturers. You can get all sorts of shapes and sizes and because they're usually painted in bright primary colours, they look really eye-catching – you could even regard one as a piece of contemporary sculpture!

Today's designs certainly bear little resemblance to the crude, rusting scaffolding once so common in the old school yard. And the most sophisticated ones are now streamlined – indeed, almost elegant – and include platforms and walkways, maybe a slide and sometimes even a playhouse.

You can include all these fun features if you make a climbing frame yourself from wood. Basically, the main structure will form a cube-shaped grid of uprights and crossbeams, but you can then use plywood or planks to fill in sections here and there and so make it more intriguing. If the frame were large enough you could turn it into a mini adventure playground by filling the central area with ropes, rope ladders and rope nets strung vertically and horizontally from the top beams.

If a full-blown climbing frame is a bit beyond your DIY capabilities you could create an equally exciting structure using the A-frame, or tent shape, idea described under playhouses for toddlers. For a climbing frame, though, only one side of the structure need be solid, and this would have horizontal struts fixed to it for climbing up to the apex. The other side of the frame could be left open but be laced with knotted ropes for really fun climbing and dangling.

A variation on the same theme would be to make an A-frame 'climb and slide' using rustic logs laid horizontally on the climbing side, and vertical logs flanking a shop-bought slide on the other side. You could even hang rope nets over the open ends of the structure – or part block them up with hardboard – to turn the inside into an adventure camp.

Depending on the design of the climbing frame, it might be possible to convert it into an attractive pergola or arbour once the children have grown up. It's certainly worth bearing this in mind from the outset as it will give you something to treasure in years to come – a sheltered retreat, smothered in scented climbers, for whiling away those lazy summer days and evenings.

Adventure swings

As children toughen up and become more independent, it does absolutely no harm to provide them with playthings that involve an element of risk. They'll respond to the challenge and will be taught to take responsibility for their own safety. With swings, all you can do is make sure that the structure itself is inherently safe – that is, that the supporting branch or frame won't collapse, the rope or chains won't break, and the seat won't fall off – and then leave the rest to them.

If at all possible, always have two swings side by side as this will encourage social interaction and be far more conducive to adventure play. Perhaps more important, it will considerably reduce the frequency of squabbles! If you haven't got a convenient branch overhanging the lawn, then construct a stout timber archway and use this instead (just make sure the uprights are adequately secured in the ground).

One popular way of making an adventure swing is to suspend an old car tyre on a rope or chain. Alternatively, you could knot a rope through a central hole in a square plank of wood, or maybe even use a wooden half-barrel. A stout log suspended between two ropes also works very well while, if you're after something really different, you could use branches or poles to make the rungs in a giant rope ladder swing. What could be easier?

Riding rough

As soon as children have got to grips with balancing on two wheels, there's just no stopping them. And with the huge surge in popularity of mountain biking, or rough stuff riding, you can expect your children to want a share of the action!

These days most kids' bikes are built to take a bit of punishment. They have extra fat tyres and sturdy frames and, generally speaking, they're far safer and easier to ride than their predecessors. So why not let your children push them to their limits and test their own skills into the bargain?

Rather than put the whole lawn at their disposal, create instead a cycle track around the perimeter. It could be attractively edged with logs or completely screened from view with plantings of tough ornamental shrubs. The children themselves can then help to create fun obstacles along the route – like logs to scramble over, ramps to jump off and posts to squeeze through – and you could even let them dig out dips or build up ridges.

Ideally, sow the whole area with a really tough variety of grass seed – maybe including some meadow grasses and flowers – and then leave it to become the wild bit of your garden. The contrast

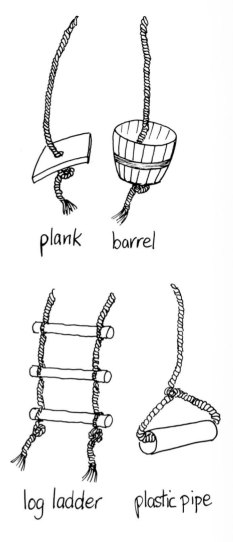

plank   barrel

log ladder   plastic pipe

25

Save wear and tear on your lawn and steer youngsters in the right direction with an attractive figure-of-eight tricycle track

Sunken tricycle track

'wild' islands

Paving bedded below turf

Ideal for younger children, this stout timber climbing frame is exciting enough in design to encourage adventure play but is not so sophisticated as to be overwhelming or frightening

between this area and your lovingly mown sward will look really stunning and the children will love you for it, as will the neighbourhood wildlife!

Ball games

There can't be a more simple, versatile and effective source of amusement than the humble ball, and so it would be a terrible shame if you were to ban ball games in the garden. Many people do, of course, fearing for the safety of their precious plants or gleaming windows. What they don't realise is that by taking just a few basic precautions, it is possible for balls, plants and windows to co-exist quite happily.

Most plants are far tougher than we imagine and, while none would appreciate being used as a punch bag, they will invariably bounce back after the occasional blow. It would make sense, though, to plant any vulnerable, treasured subjects well away from the danger zone or, alternatively, to protect them with a plant support frame or net screen – hopefully, this would take the brunt of the attack! But just as parents tend to give up on fine furnishings when they've got a house full of children, it would be much wiser to choose robust plants in the first place.

A complex climbing frame incorporating platforms, swings and camps allows for a whole range of exciting activities and will keep slightly older children amused for a good many years

27

A good deal of damage can be avoided by erecting some low trellis along the front of any borders. This will not only prevent a rolling ball from going any further, but it will also protect the edge of your lawn. And to save unnecessary trampling of plants when the children do need to retrieve a ball from the depths of the border, lay some stepping stones here and there – you'll find them handy, too, for tending plants.

Glass doesn't bounce back, of course, unless it is toughened. And while the glazing in many patio doors and conservatories is designed to resist blows – for reasons of safety and security – the average window or greenhouse remains fairly vulnerable to attack. You can reduce the risk here by encouraging ball games, whenever possible, to be played across the lawn rather than lengthways. However, as most gardens are longer than they are wide, this idea is unlikely to be met with much enthusiasm.

For complete peace of mind, it really would be worthwhile to come up with a means of protecting at least the ground floor windows and the greenhouse. And one of the simplest ways of doing this is to use lightweight plastic trellis panels, which can be hooked in place or removed in a matter of seconds. First floor windows are less likely to be in the direct line of fire and any drastic measures – like re-glazing with toughened glass or installing shutters – wouldn't really be cost-effective.

Games with nets

One way of minimising the risk of stray balls causing damage is to provide the children with a goal, or target. This way the ball games are given a sense of purpose and play can be steered in a specific direction, depending on where the net is positioned. You can buy netball and basketball posts, for example, which take up very little room, and also football goals and cricket practice nets (these could be used as fruit cages in future years).

Rebounding balls

If a ball is attached to elastic, there's absolutely no danger of the kitchen window becoming a favourite target. All sorts of rebounding bat and ball games are available from toy shops and these basically comprise a post or frame, to which a ball on an elastic line is attached, and a couple of bats. The latter could be quite small plastic ones or anything up to tennis racket size.

The great thing about games like this is that they can also be used by just one player, so children don't have to rely on always having a partner in order to amuse themselves. And if you happen to have a budding Boris Becker or Steffi Graf in the family, they're ideal for perfecting all those winning strokes!

Balls on a wall

If you're lucky enough to have an expanse of wall bordering your lawn – be it a garden wall or the side of a garage – it would be a desperate waste not to use it for ball games. So save the idea of smothering it with trellis and climbing plants for when the children have grown – which will be all too soon – and create instead some fun ideas for play.

A wall is ideal for bat and ball games but to make it more

Pell Mell

Pallemaille, pall-mall, pell-mell, mell and lawn billiards – all refer to a sport that was widely enjoyed in the seventeenth century by the nobility and rich merchants. Charles II, a real enthusiast, was largely responsible for the game's popularity. He saw it for the first time in Holland and, on his return to London, ordered a pell-mell court to be built at Whitehall Palace. But as early as the fourteenth century an English manuscript illustration shows a game being played with a hoop, balls, post and bat. By Charles' reign, it was cues rather than bats that were used and the game had a keyhole-shaped pitch with a single, pivoting iron ring at its centre. However, over the centuries there seem to have been many variations. It is generally thought that the game originated in France or Italy, *palla* meaning ball and *maglia* meaning mallet in Italian. London's Pall Mall gets its name from once being an alley where the sport was regularly played. Today just one court still exists – at the Freemason's Arms pub in Hampstead, London.

exciting you could paint a *trompe l'oeil* net on the lower half. And if you're a particularly dab hand with the paintbrush you could even include a couple of players facing you across the net!

Bouncing games are as popular today as they ever were and some, in fact, are as old as the hills. It's only the names that might change. Many have accompanying rhymes, while others involve counting and so on, and children invariably pick them up from the school playground.

You could also make up a few games, though, as children are always eager to try something new. For example, you could paint some circular targets on the wall, of varying sizes, and put a score in the middle of each – the smaller the circle, the higher the number of points. The rules could be that each player stands on a marker line and aims to score as many points as possible in, say, ten bounces. The one with the most points wins. Or, you could make it that the player who gets closest to a set number, like forty, wins and anyone who goes above that is out. Paint the circles and numbers in bright primary colours!

Rolling games
There's a host of games that involve rolling balls, either with the hand, like in the children's version of boules (sets are available from most toy departments), or with a bat, as in the centuries-old precursor to croquet, pall-mall (or pell-mell or *pallemaille*). A version of the latter is ideal for children as the rules are really simple. All you have to do is place two hoops in line with each other and a good distance apart, although this can be varied to make it more, or less, difficult. Then, starting from a marker, the player has to hit the ball, using any old mallet or bat, through both hoops. The player who takes the least number of hits to do this scores one point and, after an agreed number of rounds, the one with the most points is the winner.

Another great rolling game is skittles, which can be played using any soft ball and, say, eight empty plastic drink bottles or cartons. An easy way of playing it if there are just two participants would be to line the skittles up across the centre of the lawn and have one child at either end of the pitch so that they are facing each other. One rolls the ball, trying to knock over as many skittles as possible, and the other player then retrieves the ball to try and hit any that are still standing. The player whose throw knocks over the last of the skittles wins that round of the game and starts the next one. The loser, naturally, has to set up the skittles!

Team games
The average lawn would be hard pressed to accommodate a couple of football teams but that doesn't mean games like this need be ruled out completely. A scaled-down version of five-a-side football would be easy enough to organise and you could avoid any risk of injury or damage to the garden by using a soft ball. The pitch could be marked out with lines of sand or, if you're really serious about it, liquid white lime – the paint would grow out very quickly! Alternatively you could think up games that involve dribbling the ball (weaving in and out of posts, for example) or heading the ball from one to another.

Pot Green
In a back garden in Seaton Carew, near Hartlepool, Cleveland, the lawn has been transformed into a giant snooker table, complete with painted plastic balls, wooden cushions around the edge and pockets using old net curtains. The creator, Jimmy Murray, just wanted something a bit different on his back lawn!

Skittles
Skittles, or nine-pins, is an ancient German game called *Heidenwerfen*, meaning 'knock down pagans'. Certainly it has been played for centuries in Britain, mainly in public houses and clubs and mostly in the West of England, the Midlands, South Wales and the Lothians of Scotland. The rules and scoring varied but the basic principle was the same – that is, the bowling of a ball made of wood or rubber, weighing about 10lb, at nine oval-headed pins set in diamond formation 21ft away.

The game was exported to America in the early seventeenth century. In 1841, however, it was banned by the state of Connecticut and other states followed suit. Eventually, a tenth pin was added in order to evade the ban and that all-American sport, ten-pin bowling, was born.

Invest in a portable mini-goal and children of all ages will be able to play a game of football, or practise their scoring shots, with conviction – it will also help to steer that ball away from vulnerable plants and windows!

The simplest device, a rebounding net, can give the greatest pleasure, allowing youngsters to play at catching, kicking or heading balls to their heart's content

Another favourite team game is rounders and while officially it should be played with twenty people – ten per team – on a large pentagon-shaped pitch, it can be enjoyed in an amended form in most back gardens. Make the pitch quite small to allow enough room for fielding and, again, use a soft ball. The open palm of the hand could be used instead of a bat and, with a slight adjustment of the rules, just three children could play the game, although it would be better with more.

Buy a free-standing net like this and it can be pressed into action by kids and adults alike for a whole range of games, from volleyball to quoits to badminton – see 'The Maturing Lawn'

Cricket

Give children just a cricket bat and soft ball and they can have endless fun playing the simplest form of the game, French cricket. Here, 'fielders' surround the 'batsman', who holds the bat in an upright position to shield the legs. The object of the game is that the fielders try to throw or roll the ball so that it hits the batsman's legs. The batter counters the attack by hitting the ball away and the next throw is taken from where the ball lands – it could be just

31

Origins of the Summer Game

The earliest evidence of a game resembling cricket is a drawing dated circa 1250 which depicts two men playing with a bat and ball. And while the game is known to have been played at least as early as 1550 in Guildford, Surrey, the first recorded game was in Sussex in 1697 with eleven a side and a stake of 50 guineas. Records also show that in 1719 the Londoners (effectively, Middlesex) met the Kentish men and it is believed that this was the first match between two county sides.

At first the sport was concentrated in the southern counties, close to London, and was played on the short turf of the downs. It wasn't long before it was discovered by London society, however, and play was quickly transferred to the grounds of the sport's noble patrons in London. The most famous of all was the Artillery Ground in Finsbury.

Interestingly, a major feature of the play in those days was the heavy stake money and side bets, which depended to a large extent on very big matches. As a result, the crowds were often extremely disorderly and violently partisan!

inches away from the batsman's feet! If the legs are hit, the batter is out and the thrower takes over. The same applies if a ball is caught by a fielder. It's a great game for all the family and, what's more, it can be played on the smallest of lawns.

By providing a set of cricket stumps, the would-be Mike Gattings and Jan Brittins of this world can begin to get a taste of what real cricket is all about. But there's no need to worry at this stage about technicalities like field placings and umpires. All you need to do is mark out a pitch of, say, sixteen paces and put the bowling crease at one end, the wicket at the other.

A minimum of two can then play a simple game where the batter tries to score the most runs before being 'out', whereupon they change places. The one with the most runs at the end of the match is the winner. With more players, of course, there can be fielders and a wicket-keeper. The fielders take it in turns to bowl so many balls and when the batter is called out, the bowler – or the fielder who caused the batter to be out – takes over. A blackboard would come in handy so that the children can keep a tally of their runs.

For youngsters who want to develop their cricketing skills and enjoy the sport to the full, there is an exciting new game that has been developed by The Cricket Council and is being sponsored by the Milk Marketing Board, along with The Lord's Taverners charity. Kwik Cricket can be played by boys and girls of five and upwards and it can be as simple or complicated as they care to make it. The game can be adapted for any number of players from two to twenty-two and play can last anything from fifteen minutes to a couple of hours or more. Also, the field of play can be adjusted according to the age of the players, the chosen version of the game (five are suggested, along with rules) and the space at your disposal. Two of the games described require a pitch that is sixteen paces deep with room outside of this for fielding.

The Kwik Cricket game is being marketed by The Cricket Council (at around £50) and comprises a durable kit of two bats (in a choice of two sizes), two sets of uniquely designed stumps and two balls that are designed to lose momentum quickly so there is no danger to children or property. The equipment comes in a special hold-all, complete with a simple instruction booklet and a colourful poster. The kids will love it.

Obstacle course

Most small children have bundles of energy and need no encouragement to get plenty of healthy exercise. All too soon, however, more and more time is spent enjoying sedentary pastimes, like watching TV and playing computer games, and it becomes increasingly difficult to get them off their backsides and into that garden! The challenge is on.

Setting up an obstacle course around the perimeter of the lawn (see 'Planning a Lawn') is a great way of making exercise fun. And by allowing for an element of competition, it will keep growing children amused for years – if not the parents as well.

To allow for races, there should be either identical obstacles side by side (at least two of each) or obstacles large enough to accommodate a minimum of two children. There should also be a start and finish line – although these can be reversed, of course

– and a few basic rules, maybe even posted up on a board. If there isn't anyone to race against, the child can be timed instead.

It doesn't matter what order the obstacles are in but the more space there is between them, the better – to encourage running. And the obstacles themselves can be as zany as you like, as long as they're safe, stable and, ideally, permanent.

Climbing and jumping

If you've got a climbing frame of some description, then the object here would be to climb over the top of it as quickly as possible. If the feet touch the ground before reaching the other side, they have to start again. Then you could set up some hurdles. Saw a series of notches at regular intervals along some wooden uprights and create spikes at the ends for sinking into the turf. Then rest lengths of bamboo between the posts, adjusting the height as necessary. One rule might be that they can't proceed until they have cleared all the hurdles. Or you could say that they have to jump over one and crawl under the next one, again without knocking the bamboo off.

Balancing

Balancing beams are great fun and they also help children with co-ordination and control of their body movements. All you need are some sturdy blocks of timber at either end – they need be no more than 12in square – with a channel sawn into the upper surface to take a steel pole or a wooden beam. There is no need to make it too narrow or too long, and it will be perfectly effective just one foot off the ground.

Crawling

Tunnels to crawl through are a must in any obstacle course and one way of creating them is to get hold of some large concrete drainpipes. Failing that, you could use wooden barrels with the ends taken out. A more temporary solution would be to erect some polythene tunnel cloches, which use plastic sheeting stretched over wire hoops anchored in the ground. As long as you get ones of a reasonable diameter, it's unlikely that they will get ripped to pieces or torn out of the lawn. However, because the polythene could be dangerous, a tunnel like this should only be used if the children are supervised. Rope nets are another alternative.

Swinging

Kids love to swing from ropes Tarzan-style and so an obstacle which includes both ropes and a jump is sure to appeal to their sense of adventure. Simply build a stout timber archway and hang a couple of ropes from the crossbeam. Put markers on the grass to show where they must take off and land (if they don't clear the second marker they have to do it again!) or, alternatively, create a shallow oblong pit filled with, say, shredded bark and make this the 'no-go area'.

Pets' corner

One of the best things you can do for your children is encourage a caring and responsible attitude towards animals. And you can't

Fund-raising Fun
Instead of the children using an obstacle course simply to compete against each other for fun, why not suggest they ask members of the family, friends and neighbours to sponsor them so that they can raise money for a favourite charity? They could set themselves a reasonable target time for completing the course and ask for, say, 30p for getting around it in three minutes. Then, for every second they knock off the time a penny could be added on, for every second over the limit, a penny could be taken away. You could organise a charity sports day in your garden!

start early enough. A corner of the lawn is the ideal place to site hutches for the kids' very own pets and, by creating simple wire mesh cages as runs, everyone can share in the pleasure of observing the rabbits, guinea pigs, hamsters and so on taking their daily exercise.

Bear in mind, though, that most of these small mammals need to be taken inside – or at least into the shed or garage – during the colder months of the year. Make sure the cage is reasonably portable but at the same time good and sturdy to guard against cat or fox attack. The same goes for the run, which must be securely anchored to the lawn.

Older children, as well as adults, could get enormous pleasure

For minimum outlay a cricket set will provide hours of amusement for all ages, whether playing strictly by the rules or simply devising fun versions of the game

An obstacle course can be as challenging and sophisticated as you or the children care to make it, but that doesn't mean you need anything special in the way of equipment – with a little ingenuity, everyday household items would serve equally well

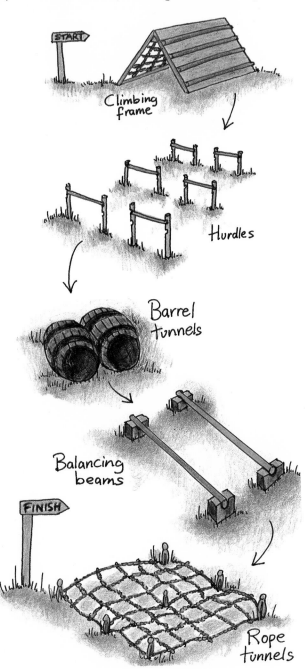

34

Encourage children to have pets and they can use a sheltered corner of the lawn to site hutches and runs and so forth. Always put the needs of the animals first, though, and be prepared to take ultimate responsibility for their welfare

from keeping cage birds and an attractive aviary sited on the lawn looks, and sounds, really charming. Again, watching the occupants – be they canaries, budgies, foreign finches or parrots – will provide hours of amusement for the whole family.

Aviaries can be bought from shops or you can make one yourself just as long as you check out the birds' requirements first of all. There is no shortage of books on the subject. Needless to say, though, you shouldn't embark on a project like this unless you are prepared to take ultimate responsibility for the welfare of your offspring's feathered friends – and the same applies to all pets of course.

The best site for an aviary will be relatively quiet and sheltered but not underneath a tree. And to be practical it will need to be

Let budding thespians indulge their every whim with an outdoor theatre. It would be simplicity itself to set up and would make an intriguing focal point on the lawn – see 'On the stage'

35

about head height to allow easy access for cleaning, feeding and so on. The part that is enclosed will need a wood or concrete floor, but the ground in the flying area can be left as lawn – it would only be ruined if you were to keep ground living birds like quail or bantam.

The keeping of certain pets can become an all-consuming hobby and pastime. It can also be extremely educational. And you never know, if you have a budding Gerald Durrell in the family, before long your lawn could be turned into a veritable safari park!

Off the shelf

Go to any toy department in a local store and you will usually find at least a Wendy house, a range of bat and ball games and maybe even a basic swing or slide. Go to a specialist toy shop, though, and you'll find it's an Aladdin's cave of outdoor games and activities. The selection is mind boggling and, even better news, most of the items are highly affordable – around the £15 mark (the price of a couple of garden shrubs) or less.

For example, there is a really impressive croquet set for children (and probably perfectly suitable for adults as well!), which comes neatly packed on a sturdy two-wheeled trolley. And there is something called a Slippy slide, which will give little ones hours of fun on hot summer days as they slither and splash their way along a polythene chute covered in water. A slight improvement on the average garden sprinkler!

If the idea of digging up your lawn to create a sandpit doesn't appeal, you can buy an Activity Sandpit, which is a moulded plastic unit with sunken areas and compartments for sand, water and so on. Or if you want to give your toddler a swing and you don't fancy the DIY bit, you can choose from a whole range of specially designed cradle seats.

For the adventure playground there are various ready-made devices on offer, all at very reasonable prices. You can get a trapeze bar and rope ladder, for example, and also something called a Twizzler – it's fixed to the end of a rope and the child dangles in the air, spinning this way and that!

The lawn, of course, is the only place where certain toys can be played with, realistically. One of these is the old favourite, stilts, and they can still be found propped up in many a toy shop, just begging to be bought. Another is the more recent invention, the Bopper Hopper ball, on which toddlers and youngsters (and undoubtedly the occasional adult too) can sit and bounce their way fairly uncontrollably all around the garden.

On a similar theme – bouncing, that is – you could buy a trampoline for the kids. At around £100, it would be a good deal more expensive than any of the other ideas, but then a trampoline isn't simply a toy or game. It's likely to give many years of enjoyment, for children of all ages, and prove an invaluable form of exercise, strengthening muscles and teaching co-ordination.

On the stage

Some might rather unfairly call them show-offs but, in fact, a good many children have a perfectly healthy desire to perform to an audience, whether it's to sing a simple nursery rhyme, play on a recorder or stage a full blown ballet. Putting on a show is a favourite pastime for stage-struck youngsters and, weather permitting, there's no better place for it than on the lawn.

So why not give them a permanent theatre – somewhere for them to rehearse, give performances and simply have fun? It is easy enough to do. Position the 'stage' so that the back of it can be a boundary wall or fence. Frame the front with a wide archway – grow climbing plants over it if you like – and erect free-standing 'flaps' on both sides using, say, trellis panels. That way there is an element of surprise for the audience as the performers suddenly appear from the wings.

Alternatively, a gazebo, pergola or arbour could be pressed into action, as long as it is big enough. The most important thing is that the children have a defined space, preferably framed, which will fire their imagination and give the impression of a real theatre. And for the performance proper, if you can help them to rig up some sort of curtain and maybe some scenery painted on, say, lengths of lining paper, all the better.

A final thought if you have a terraced or sloping lawn is the possibility of creating tiered seating – maybe in a semi-circle – with a 'stage' at a lower level. Not only would the children have their very own amphitheatre but you would have a ready-made setting for entertaining friends and holding garden parties.

Seasonal games

A threatening cloud or two and the odd spot of rain may send adults scurrying into the house, but children are made of far tougher stuff. They would much rather brave the elements than give up on a favourite pastime, and why not? Suitably dressed, there is no reason why children shouldn't be out playing in all but the very worst of weathers.

Most of the games and pastimes discussed so far will keep youngsters amused not just in the summer months but all year round. Indeed, adventure swings and so on are positively

Seasonal games

leaf sculpture

snow city

improved by the addition of a little wind and wet. But with the changing seasons comes the chance to devise more specific activities – ones that will be looked forward to and treasured just because they are so transient.

Autumn leaves
As autumn approaches, so you will be facing the seemingly endless chore of clearing fallen leaves from the lawn. So why not do yourself a favour and turn the job into an irresistible activity for kids? Younger children will have lots of fun collecting them by the bucketful and building a heap, and you could even make it into a race to see who ends up with the biggest pile. As a reward, before you finally put the leaves into plastic bags, you could let the children spend some time throwing themselves into their very own multi-coloured mountain.

Alternatively, as an inducement to clearing the leaves away, they could first use them to create giant pictures and sculptures on the lawn. And by using them to draw lines, they could make pitches for ball games or hopscotch. Older children could pack the leaves straight into tough plastic bin liners and make handy punch bags or cushions for their camp!

Snow
All you need is a sprinkling of snow for children to discover the delights of snowball fights and snowmen. But the fun doesn't stop there. Wrapped up warm and well shod, youngsters can experiment with any number of ball games on a lawn covered with snow, and that novel texture – slippy one minute, soft the next – will only add to their amusement. If any pitches are needed, they can scrape through the snow at will to create stark green lines.

If several inches have fallen, the children can embark on some major landscaping work. They could dig out sweeping troughs to use as chutes and slides or even build an ice rink by tamping down a circle of snow. Younger children could build castles, cars, boats and monsters – as they would out of sand – while older ones could have competitions to sculpt, say, the tallest totem pole. Then the whole family could get together to create a miniature village or fantasy landscape and, hopefully, complete it before the thaw!

THE MATURING LAWN

How many supposedly responsible adults can say that on seeing a deserted playground they haven't been sorely tempted to have a go on that super-duper slide or wonderful witch's hat? If the truth were known, not many! For the sake of appearances, we resist the temptation and go on our way, secretly bemoaning the injustice of it all – why should children have all the fun? But while we might be disinclined to indulge in play in public – apart from organised sports, that is – there's no earthly reason why we shouldn't let our hair down in the privacy of our own back garden. Forget that playground and turn to your lawn!

Unless you're extremely thick-skinned, you will probably draw the line at the idea of investing in swings and slides for your own amusement. After all, visiting friends and colleagues are unlikely to be that understanding! But you can get just as much fun from a host of perfectly acceptable games and activities. The knack, in many cases, is to disguise play with a sense of purpose!

Teenagers will be particularly appreciative of this inventive, if not somewhat devious, approach to recreation. Stuck self-consciously between childhood and adulthood, they'd be the last ones to admit they have a hankering for schoolyard games, yet their still boundless energy is hardly satisfied by so-called grown-up pursuits – perhaps, at best, a game of cards or chess!

So the absence of young children in the family is no excuse for not having fun in the garden. That expanse of lawn is just begging to be used as an outdoor room. Not simply for sitting in (that comes later) but for a whole load of action and amusement. If you're a fitness fanatic, it can be your gymnasium. If you're a sports enthusiast, it can be your arena. You can play games that test your every skill or, just as skilfully, you can avoid those ones like the plague. The beauty of it is that you can do exactly as you please.

And just because your lawn is to become a hive of activity doesn't mean you have to give up on the idea of having an attractive garden. Any permanent pieces of equipment you may wish to include – like, say, parallel bars or vaults for a work-out – can, with just a little imagination, be made into perfectly acceptable, aesthetically pleasing features. Alternatively, strategically placed plantings and screens can work wonders if you're after out and out camouflage (see 'Structures and Special Features').

To get the best all-round use out of your lawn, though, you should aim to set aside as big an area as possible for playing games. If space allows, confine gym equipment and so on to the perimeter. Otherwise, opt for portable or easily dismantled items. However serious you might be about keeping fit, it would be a fearful waste to have a lawn and not be able to indulge in at least the occasional game of clock golf or croquet!

Victorian Values

The heyday of the British lawn was in Victorian times. The advent of the mower, invented in 1832, meant the grass could be kept neat and tidy without laborious scything and anyone with a garden, however small, cultivated and took pride in their patch of grass. The Victorians entertained themselves at home and, naturally enough, their activities moved on to the lawn. It was a place to sit and relax, take tea and play all manner of games, including croquet, cricket and tennis.

This is how gardens continued to be used until the early part of this century. Then, two things happened. World War I saw many lawns being dug up in order to grow much needed fresh vegetables (and even more so during World War II) and the advent of the motorcar meant that more and more people were able to find entertainment away from the home.

The latter continued to be the norm for several decades but, thankfully, all that is now changing. Few car owners find travelling a pleasure and, as a result, the home and garden are once again becoming the focal points for entertainment, recreation and relaxation. Of the many much maligned Victorian values, the return to this one must surely be welcomed!

First Boules

Games involving the throwing of hefty balls at a jack can be traced back to the ancient Egyptians, Romans and Greeks and one theory is that it may well have been the Roman legionnaires who first introduced a game like this into the Provence area of France. In these earliest days the balls were probably large stones, since the main purpose of the activity was to build up the soldiers' or athletes' strength.

Nevertheless, through the ages its popularity as a game continued to grow, although still largely amongst soldiers and sailors; the French King Charles V even tried to ban it because it was proving so distracting. But with stones, and later cannon balls, so readily to hand any attempts to stop the game were futile. By the seventeenth century the game was widespread and it's even said that it was boules, not bowls, that Sir Francis Drake was playing that day on Plymouth Hoe.

By the latter half of the nineteenth century a game called *Jeu Provençale* was being widely enjoyed in the South of France. It used smaller balls over a shorter distance, yet it still demanded a good deal of stamina and strength. Then, in 1910, a man called Ernest Pitiot devised a slightly less demanding version, with a throwing distance of just six metres, for a friend and enthusiast whose health was failing. Now players could stand still to throw the balls and, as a result, the game became hugely popular with people of all ages. Its name, *pétanque*, came from the expression that originally made fun of Pitiot's new game – *pieds tanques*, meaning 'feet tied together'!

Boules

The French game of boules, or pétanque to be precise, can be played on every imaginable surface – except grass, that is! So say the British Pétanque Association and who are we to argue with them. It would seem, then, that the game of boules should be excluded from these pages, but such is its popularity that not to mention the feasibility of playing the game in your garden would be a sad and conspicuous omission.

For some the mention of the game immediately conjures up visions of a boulevard or village square in the warmer climes of southern France with portly beretted Frenchmen in quiet contemplation under the shade of a tree, escaping the heat of the day. But the truth is that boules has now become a game for all, all over the world, and it is being taken up with enthusiasm, be it in the garden of the pub or down on the beach.

The reason grass is not suitable is that an essential aspect of the game is the unpredictability of how the boules will react on the surface. A loose material like gravel or stony earth is ideal as it has plenty of undulations and is rough enough to stop the boules rolling too far. Also, its inherent instability means the nature of the pitch (or *terrain* or *piste*) will alter during the course of a game, so heightening the challenge.

For serious pétanque players, then, grass is out of the question. So if you want to do more than simply play a fun version of the game using a set of plastic boules from a toy shop – the real ones are metal and made to exacting specifications – it would be worthwhile creating a tailor-made pitch within your lawn. This is easily done and it can be made to look extremely attractive given a decorative edging of, say, brick or timber.

All you have to do is excavate a strip of lawn at least 12m long and 1.5m wide (the official size of a pitch) to a depth of about 5in. Infill with an inch or so of crushed hardcore, well bedded down and rolled, and top-dress the whole area with about half an inch of gravel or similar material. A final rolling will finish the job off nicely. Don't worry about the pitch being dead flat, as a slope only adds to the fun.

Boules can be played as singles (two people), doubles (four people) or triples (three people per side). With the latter, each player has two boules to play with, while for singles and doubles the player has three. Good quality competition boules can be bought from sports shops and specialist suppliers, and in order to get the most out of the game it is worthwhile going for the best – for a set of three, expect to pay no less than about £25 and anything up to £40 or so. The only other equipment you'll need is a carrier for the boules (from as little as £5), a jack or *cochonnet* (a matter of pence) and a measure (from just a couple of pounds up to about £10 or more for a specialist one).

Finally, remember that boules is also a tremendous spectator sport. So provide some bench seating on the lawn around your pitch and it will be appreciated by players and on-lookers alike!

Croquet

These days you would be hard pressed to find even the remnants of a cucumber sandwich amongst the thousands of committed croquet players up and down the country – a pint of beer, yes, and maybe a barbecued burger! Long gone are the days when croquet was a sport for the idle rich. It's now being enjoyed in back gardens, large and small, in parks, sports clubs and even school playgrounds. In fact, anywhere there is a patch of turf.

Today's national champions had their first introduction to croquet in just such humble surroundings and, indeed, the first rounds of the annual championships are still held on domestic lawns. At competition level, the official size of the court is 28yd by 35yd, which admittedly is about seven times the size of the average garden lawn, but the game can be played on a much smaller scale and be equally enjoyable and challenging.

The idea of croquet being a test of skill and strategy is likely to come as some surprise to the uninitiated. Of course, you can devise simplified versions of the game for casual amusement – and for the whole family to enjoy – but the sport in its proper form is as complex and mentally demanding as a game of bridge and as physically exacting as a game of snooker.

You can buy croquet sets in sports shops and in the games departments of larger stores. Basically, they will comprise four mallets, four balls, hoops and a peg. The rules will be included, of course, which will at least enable you to get off to a reasonably good start. Be warned, though, that as you become increasingly hooked on the game, so you will undoubtedly want to develop your skills and your knowledge.

To that end, it would be worthwhile buying the best croquet set you can afford – that click of wooden mallet on ball isn't quite the same when it's plastic! – and investigating the possibility of joining a local croquet club. There are around two hundred at the moment, with more springing up all the time, and by becoming a member you can meet fellow enthusiasts and always be sure of someone to play with. Also, many of the clubs offer evening classes to teach you the rudimentary skills of the game. Who knows, next year you could be croqueting with champions!

Quoits
The mention of quoits is likely to conjure up one of two distinctly different pictures – that of rubber rings being thrown over a net or metal rings being thrown over a post. Both games are commonly called quoits, although the former is perhaps better known as deck tennis and the latter is more usually played these days as horseshoes. Confusing, maybe, but the important thing is that they are equally perfect for playing on your lawn.

Deck tennis has been popular on board ship and in gardens for decades and the great thing about the game is that it can be played in a very limited space. All you need is a net 4ft 8in high strung across the centre of a rectangular court – this can be any size, as can the quoit. You need to mark out a 'neutral zone', which extends 3ft into the court on either side of the net, but that done you're ready for action.

The game is intended for two or four players and it involves throwing the quoit across the net to be caught one-handed by an opponent who, in turn, immediately returns the quoit with the same hand and from the exact catch point. A point is won when

Going through the Hoops
It is generally thought that croquet evolved from the game of *pallemaille* or pell-mell, which is known to have been played in France as early as the thirteenth century (see 'The Growing Up Lawn – ball games'). Using the same basic elements, croquet was a far more complicated and sophisticated sport, using six or more hoops as opposed to just one or two, and by the mid-1800s it was in its heyday in England, being played in gardens large and small at every opportunity. By 1870 its popularity had spread all over the United States and in the same year the All England Croquet Club was formed. Their grounds were in Wimbledon. For the next couple of decades, however, croquet had to play second fiddle to the up and coming sport of lawn tennis, which also became an all-consuming craze. But croquet saw a revival in around 1894 and The United All England Croquet Association (now The Croquet Association, based at the Hurlingham Club, London SW6) was formed a couple of years later.

The experts say boules mustn't be played on grass but there's no reason why you shouldn't create a special pitch and make an attractive feature of it within your lawn. Here are three different styles of edging

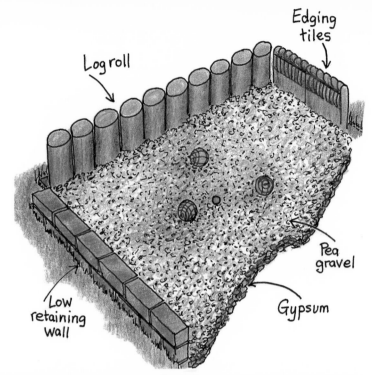

Log roll

Edging tiles

Low retaining wall

Pea gravel

Gypsum

The most traditional of garden games, croquet, can be enjoyed by all the family, whether to provide fun entertainment or to test the players' every skill

the opponent fails to return the quoit into the court, and a point is lost if the quoit lands in the neutral zone. The first side to reach fifteen points wins a set, and the first side to win two out of three sets (or three out of five) wins the game.

Originally, the quoit used for the game described above was made of rope, which is a far cry from the quoit defined in *Chambers Dictionary* as 'a heavy flat ring for throwing as near as possible to a hob or pin'. This version of quoits is closely related to Horseshoe Pitching, which originated in North America in colonial times. In fact, a national association was formed back in 1926 and every year there are national and world championships in the sport.

The game of horseshoes differs from quoits in that play takes place between two steel stakes, 14in high, placed some 30ft to 40ft apart. Each stake is positioned in the centre of a 6ft square pitching box – this can be marked out with string and pegs – and is set so that it tilts slightly towards the other. Two players pitch from one box to the other, throwing two shoes each, which is called an inning. Then they walk to the opposite box and pitch from that.

Scores are taken after each inning. Three points are scored for each ringer (encircling the stake) and one point for each shoe closer than an opponent's as long as it is within 6in of the stake. No points are scored in the event of ties and it is the first player to reach a score of twenty-one that wins. With four players, each pair of partners pitches from opposite boxes.

Volleyball

Watch a top-level game of volleyball and the chances are you'll be mesmerised – it's certainly hard to beat in the excitement stakes. But play a game yourself and the chances are you'll be well and truly hooked – it is one of the most satisfying team games around and, what's more, it is dead easy to set up.

A proper game of volleyball requires six players per side and a court measuring 59ft by 29ft 6in, but it can be played equally successfully in a smaller space and with fewer people. Even for an informal game, though, you should ideally have an 'attacking line' a few feet back on either side of the net. The latter should be 3ft 3in deep and suspended so that the top edge is 4ft 8in above the court. Any soft ball will do although, again ideally, it should be just slightly smaller than that used for basketball.

Strictly speaking, each half of the court should be divided into six sections, which allows the players to rotate their position, according to the rules. But this is hardly necessary for a knock-about game on the lawn. All you really have to know is that the ball can only be hit with your palm or fist and that the aim is to hit the ball onto the ground in your opponents' court. You will soon see that, even in its most simple form, the game can be a real test of skill, strategy and stamina. For a few tips, though, why not visit a local sportsclub.

Archery

It would be a great shame if such a venerable sport and pastime as archery were to fall into disrepute simply as a result of bad press caused by an irresponsible minority. Its history goes back some

Exercise for Businessmen
Volleyball was invented in 1895 by William G. Morgan at the YMCA gymnasium in Holyoke, Massachusetts. Originally called mintonette, Morgan had wanted to design an indoor sport for those businessmen who found the new game of basketball rather too vigorous. Whether they took to it or not, the game soon spread all over America. However, The Amateur Volleyball Association of Great Britain was only formed in 1955.

Once as popular as croquet, the sport of archery these days tends to be confined to clubs. If you have a good-sized lawn, though, responsible adults could certainly give it a try – just make sure you get advice from the experts

Darts

While archery demands a fairly large lawn, even the smallest patch can accommodate darts. And imagine how much more pleasant, and safer, it would be to take the game outside. A far cry indeed from the typical image of beer-swilling players amidst a haze of cigarette smoke! The board could be fixed to a tree, using a makeshift timber frame constructed around the trunk – don't nail directly into the bark! – or you could devise a free-standing easel-type structure, similar to that used for archery. A child's blackboard and easel could be used for keeping score. One word of warning, though. However good a shot you are, keep young children and pets well away and don't fix the board to a boundary fence – stray arrows won't amuse the neighbours!

There's little evidence of darts being played as an organised game prior to the twentieth century, although the concept probably originates from the days when archers used weighted ten-inch arrows in self-defence while fighting at close-quarters. 'Dartes' are known to have been used in Ireland in the sixteenth century and a form of the game was apparently played on the *Mayflower* in 1620 by the Plymouth Pilgrims.

Saturday, 16 July 1870

'The party divided itself into croquet and archery. High tea at seven just before which someone managed to shoot a chicken with an arrow, or it was said so, and Margaret Oswald told me that as I put my head through the railings to rake a croquet ball out of the field on to the lawn, my head looked so tempting that she felt greatly inclined to shoot at it. Certainly there would have been this comfort, that if she had shot at me I should have been very much safer than if she had not, because wherever else the arrow might have gone it certainly would not have hit me.'

REVEREND FRANCIS KILVERT *Kilvert's Diary*

ten thousand years and, in England, the oldest sporting contest to date is the Ancient Scorton Silver Arrow, which first took place in 1673. Indeed, archery was enjoyed by the masses for centuries and, until relatively recently, it was also a favourite garden game.

There seems to be no good reason why responsible adults shouldn't continue to enjoy archery for at least another few centuries. And you can help to get the arrows flying, so to speak, by taking up the challenge on your very own lawn. Just remember, though, that a bow and arrow, however rudimentary or sophisticated, is a potentially lethal weapon and, as such, should be treated with due care and respect. Certainly keep them well away from children.

An important aspect of traditional bows is that the pull, which is measured in pounds' weight, varies according to their size. Usually, the taller and stronger the player, the greater the pull required and, in turn, the bigger the bow and the further the arrow will travel. It follows, therefore, that by choosing a particular size of bow you can determine quite exactly the range over which you can shoot and, by placing the target well within this, you can be safe in the knowledge that arrows will not stray outside the specified area. This is vital in domestic back gardens, of course, and it shows just how necessary it is to get expert advice first.

The target for archery is reminiscent of a giant straw place mat, coloured gold in the centre and surrounded by rings of red, blue, black and white, finishing with an outside border of green. Standard targets – which would normally be placed anything from fifty to a hundred yards away – are 4ft in diameter and can be purchased from major sports shops and specialist manufacturers. They are supported on a sort of easel.

For the record, you score nine for hitting the gold band, seven for the red, five for the blue, three for the black and one for the white. The player with the greatest number of points after shooting an agreed number of arrows is the winner.

Golf

You can practise your swings and strokes to your heart's content if you invest in a practice ball – it just won't go anywhere. Then you can polish up on your putting technique by simply sinking a plastic pot or beaker into the lawn and keeping the surrounding area closely mown. For experienced golfers and novices alike, having a lawn, where they can do their homework unhindered, will save many a blush at the eighteenth hole out on the golf course!

But golf is a game that can be enjoyed by all, at any level, and with a lawn at your disposal you can forget about having to join clubs, make bookings or fawn to fellow members! A really fun version of the game, for example, is Clock Golf, which has the simplest of rules but is capable of rousing the greatest of passions. With a central hole in the lawn, twelve teeing-off stations are marked at each hour of a circular clock – the radius can be as great as space allows. The object of the game is that players take it in turns to pot the ball from each point and the one who completes the circuit in the fewest number of putts is declared the winner. Sharing just one club and ball, there's no limit to the number of people who can play the game.

By creating several holes at strategic places around the lawn it is possible to have your own mini golf course. And you can make it even more fun by planning each hole so that it includes at least one obstacle – say, an island bed or a small sand-filled bunker – that players must endeavour to avoid. You could continue this theme, of course, and set up a crazy golf course, in which case you would have a whole series of obstacles to negotiate, like ramps, drainpipes, pits and hummocks – maybe even water. The object, as always, would be to get around the course in the fewest number of strokes.

Badminton

Of all sports, badminton must be the one best suited to being played on the garden lawn. The court measures just 44ft by 20ft and because you are using a shuttlecock instead of a ball – as in tennis, say – there is no danger of causing damage to the garden or house windows.

With a little help from someone in the know, you can pick up the rules and a few basic techniques in no time at all. Then, as long as you have a reasonably keen eye, you can continue to enjoy the game right up to the highest level. The only likely killjoy would be the wind.

To play the game seriously you will have to mark out the court and the only really effective way of doing this is with whitewash from a traditional roller dispenser. Plot the lines first, using string and pegs, to make sure they are accurate and straight.

The net for badminton should be 2ft 6in deep, with the top edge 5ft off the ground in the centre of the court and 5ft 1in at the posts. It should be edged with a 3in band of white tape. You will have to buy rackets and shuttlecocks, of course, but relatively cheap ones will probably be perfectly adequate.

Table tennis

While strictly speaking an indoor game, the majority of us are far more likely to be able to accommodate a game of table tennis on our lawn than in our living room. And this will be particularly true if, like the professionals, the players have visions of conducting rallies some six feet back from the table!

There is absolutely no reason why ping-pong shouldn't be played outside just as long as it isn't too windy. And like tennis and badminton, it's a game that will test your skill and give you hours of amusement – all, what's more, for a relatively small initial outlay in terms of money and effort.

It is possible to buy a purpose-built table but it would be simplicity itself to make your own. The overall dimensions of the playing surface should be 9ft long by 5ft wide and it should be made of 1in thick solid wood – it would be more manageable, of course, to have two 4ft 6in by 5ft sections that can be clamped together. These can then be supported 2ft 6in off the ground by, say, a stout trestle table. Finish off the playing surface with a coat of dark paint and edge it with a ¾in white line. For doubles, you also need a white line down the middle of the table.

You can buy a net – along with the rackets and balls – from any good games or sports shop but, for the record, it should be 6ft

Be a real professional and create proper golf holes within the lawn

Palas

Palas is a popular beach game in France and Spain, which hasn't as yet reached the shores of Britain – which is a shame since it would also be perfect for the lawn. Hopefully it won't be too long before we see palas sets for sale in the UK. Like tennis, the game is played by either two or four people who volley a ball back and forth. But there any similarity ends. There is no court as such, no net and no real rules.

The palas racquet is a paddle-shaped bat, with a shortish handle, made from one piece of solid wood. Understandably they're not particularly light, although three sizes/weights are available. Be warned, the heaviest is certainly quite a handful! The object of the game is to keep the tennis-type ball in play for as long as possible without it touching the ground – and on soft sand, of course, it wouldn't bounce anyway. But to this end, rather than trying to beat your opponent with fancy passing shots and so on (the temptation is enormous), you have to work together to control the ball and keep it going, counting the number of volleys in each rally.

Opposing players can be as far apart as they like and, obviously, the closer they are, the faster the game.

45

Badminton can be enjoyed on any average-sized lawn as the shuttlecock will never stray too far however hard you hit it. And there's no need to worry about the complexities of court markings – for a fun game you can simply rely on fancy shots and smashes to thrash your opponents

long (fixed 6in outside the table on either side by means of clamps) and 6¾in high, the bottom edge resting on the table.

Lawn tennis

There's nothing to stop you stringing up a simple net across the lawn for a knock-about game of tennis. But to play lawn tennis proper you would have to be able to accommodate a court measuring 78ft by 36ft (27ft for singles) and you would probably need to provide some sort of net enclosure to prevent the ball constantly going astray. That said, if you have got the space, the initial effort required to set up your very own permanent court would be amply rewarded.

There aren't many lawns that can accommodate a proper tennis court but few are too small for some form of swing-ball device. A great idea for a casual, knock-about game or for getting to grips with those winning strokes

As with badminton you would have to mark out the court with whitewashed lines, which will need to be repainted at regular intervals. The posts that support the net should be 3ft 6in high and should be positioned 3ft outside the court on either side. The net at the central point must be exactly 3ft off the ground.

If lack of space makes it impossible for you to play conventional tennis on your lawn, you could opt instead for a game where the ball is attached to an elastic line on a post. The rules of play are usually quite specific, so you can make the game as challenging and competitive as you like. Alternatively, you can use the device to simply brush up on that backhand.

Lawn board games

Just because your idea of a worthwhile game might be more concerned with contemplative strategy than physical exertion doesn't mean you can't play it in the great outdoors. Of course, you can set up any board game on a garden table, but create a giant-size version of, say, chess or draughts on your lawn and it will take on a totally new dimension, in every sense. The giant board will allow you to exercise rather more than your wrist action and others to enjoy a view of the play. Immediately the game becomes a sociable pursuit that can be enjoyed by players and spectators alike.

To make a giant game yourself you first of all need to think about the board. This could be made from two sheets of 8ft by 4ft hardboard, hinged together and painted with the required sixty-four contrasting squares. Or you could make a striking permanent feature of the board by setting paving slabs or brick setts into your lawn so that alternate squares are left as grass.

The pieces can be as sophisticated as your carpentry skills allow. For chess, the simplest way would be to form cylinders (thirty-two of them) from flexible plywood or the like and paint these with the appropriate distinguishing features – a horse's head, a king and queen's crown, a bishop's mitre and so on. For

Tennis on the lawn was a popular activity in Victorian and Edwardian days, though the players' outfits did little to speed up the rallies

One innovative company produces a range of high quality, giant board games, all of which are ideal for playing on the lawn

Live Chess

Why not have a chess party? A minimum of thirty-four people (thirty-two 'pieces' and two 'players') can be given appropriate head-dresses – pawns, bishops, knights, kings, queens, etc – and invited to take part in a giant chess game on the lawn. Mark out the squares with tape or mown stripes and divide the guests into two teams. One person on each side can be the player, maybe liaising with the 'pieces' as play develops, or each piece can be a player for one move. Impose time limits to ensure play is fast moving!

draughts, any sort of discs (you want twenty-four) would suffice – even up-turned plastic plant tubs – as long as they are relatively light. Don't forget to paint half the pieces in a contrasting colour!

If the do-it-yourself bit doesn't appeal you'll be pleased to hear that you can now buy giant sets of draughts and chess from a specialist firm. The board is made from sixty-four interlocking tiles, each 1ft square, and the pieces are attractively moulded – the largest chess piece is 2ft high while the draughts are 10in across. Mini-giant versions are available if space is restricted (the board is then 4ft square). Other giant board games on offer are Tic-Tac-Toe (noughts and crosses) measuring 3ft square and Shuffleboard measuring 14ft by 3ft. The latter is an old game similar in principle to shove-halfpenny.

Shaping up

Turning your lawn into a gymnasium isn't such a far-fetched idea. OK, you might not be an aspiring gymnast, but there's nothing to stop you at least investing in a keep fit tape so that you can don your personal hi-fi – or put the speakers at an open window – and have a daily work-out in the fresh air. If you can get some friends, or the rest of the family, to join you, all the better!

With a lawn at your disposal you can grab some exercise at the drop of a hat, even for just a few minutes, and you can take it as seriously as you please. The only factor that might affect your enthusiasm for the idea is the proximity of your neighbours – unless, that is, you're an exhibitionist by nature! – but then you can always put paid to prying eyes with a few strategically placed ornamental screens.

If you've got a pocket handkerchief of a lawn, using it as a circuit for jogging will probably sound too ridiculous for words. But on a more serious note, women in particular might well consider this a far safer and more attractive alternative to running alone on the streets. So, as long as your lawn is of a reasonable size – preferably incorporating some interesting contours and features for added stimulation – why not give it a try? Draw up a circular route and aim to complete so many laps per session, setting yourself higher targets each week or timing yourself against the clock. You could devise some sort of lap marker – either a clock with a pointer or a numbered flip-chart – that could be fixed to a post and altered each time you pass by. And you could make the circuit all the more challenging by setting up the odd obstacle, like a hurdle or balancing beam, along the way – it could become a veritable assault course!

If you already have some specialised exercise equipment like, say, a rowing machine or bicycle, there's no reason why you shouldn't set it up on the lawn. But if you were to leave it out permanently, of course, it would soon get rusted to bits. Far better, then, to build some basic equipment that will stand up to the elements and be ready and waiting whenever you want to use it. No great DIY skills are needed, just a little inventiveness.

Returning to the idea of screens for privacy, you can kill two birds with one stone by creating a free-standing structure with horizontal rungs from top to bottom – remember the sort of thing that lined the walls of the school gymnasium? This could be pressed into action for a whole variety of exercises, especially those involving isometrics, which is where the muscles are flexed when they are in a fixed positon – for example, pushing against a bar or pulling backwards. Alternatively, you could hang from the rungs by your arms, with your back to the screen, and do leg-raises and body-raises. Or you could hook your legs over a rung and do sit-ups hanging upside down!

On this note, most gyms these days have equipment that allows you to do sit-ups and so forth while lying on an angled bench – the more acute the angle, the more demanding the exercise. You could make something along the same lines by knocking up an oblong timber platform and fixing sturdy hooks to one end. Ideally, lay some padding over the top, covering it with PVC or vinyl, and remember to incorporate a rubber strap at the hook end for anchoring the feet. Then you can simply hang the bench over one of the rungs of your screen to get the angle you require.

Weight training is a popular form of exercise for men and women alike and, while it shouldn't be undertaken without expert guidance, once you know what you are doing you can work-out in the privacy of your back garden to your heart's content. And you will need hardly any specialist equipment. Indeed, the very lightest of weights – like a couple of house bricks, say – can have the most marked effect on a few basic exercises. Buy a good book on the subject or go for a few lessons and you'll also discover that just a simple bench is one of the main requirements. This should be wide enough to support your shoulders, long enough to take your head and torso, and at a height that will allow you to keep your feet on the ground when you are lying back with your knees over the end. The sloping bench, as described above, would also come in handy.

Ropes suspended from a robust archway or branch will allow you to strengthen muscles by climbing and swinging and so on. Of course, you might want to show off your gymnastic expertise on a pair of rings, but bear in mind that they ought to be over 8ft from the ground! Parallel bars, high bars and asymmetric bars are a far more realistic proposition and these would also be fairly easy to build. Or how about a pommel horse or a punch bag?

Nature watch

Unless you live in the heart of the country, it is your garden that will bring you closest to Mother Nature. Searching out wildlife – and even actively encouraging it – is a fascinating pastime and one that can be endlessly enjoyed right outside your back door. If you've ever had the joy of watching a fox basking in the autumn sunshine slap bang in the middle of your lawn, you won't need any further persuasion!

The best managed gardens, with close mown lawns and well weeded flower beds, may win you the admiration of your neighbours but will do little to tempt the local wildlife population to take up residence. Creating a wild garden means throwing traditional gardening methods to the wind and adopting a totally different approach – one that centres not on maintenance but on decay and a certain amount of neglect. Sounds drastic, maybe, but believe it or not, the end result can be as attractive as any neatly

What could be better than a work-out
in the fresh air, right on your doorstep
– no tedious travelling to the local gym,
no bookings, no club fees. The
apparatus is ready and waiting
whenever you want to use it

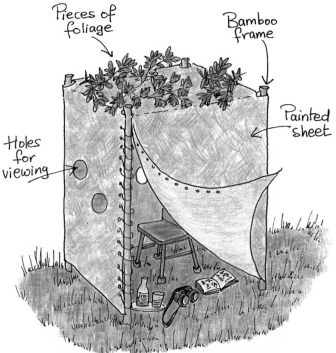

Pieces of
foliage

Bamboo
frame

Painted
sheet

Holes
for
viewing

First take appropriate steps to
encourage wildlife to your garden and
then set up your very own hide to
observe the new residents at your
leisure

Make-shift wildlife hide

Grace your lawn with a charming dovecote or bird-table and you'll have a constant source of pleasure and amusement. Note how this one sits atop a tree stump smothered with vegetation – a perfect habitat for all manner of fascinating creepy crawlies and even certain small mammals

manicured plot and it will certainly be more intriguing.

You can make a great start by sacrificing just a few square yards of your carefully nurtured lawn to turn it over to meadow. Yes, just a small patch of turf, left to its own devices until around about June – and maybe sown with a mixture of meadow grasses and flowers just to get it off to a flying start – will attract a host of wonderful little creatures such as butterflies, grasshoppers, ladybirds and dragonflies, to name but a few. Come harvest time, use a nylon line trimmer, shears or scythe to cut the hay, which must be shaken vigorously to scatter all the wildflower seeds lurking within and then removed to the compost heap or vegetable plot. Remember to keep the grass adjacent to your meadow neatly mown and the effect will be truly charming.

There are several excellent books that explain how to go about creating a wildlife garden. Done properly, you can look forward to many happy hours of nature watching, be it with binoculars from the window or – and it's not such a far-fetched idea – at closer quarters from your very own hide. Simply allocate an area of your garden to become a wildlife reserve, preferably furthest away from the house, and set up a small hut or makeshift camp on the edge of your lawn. Camouflage it with quick-growing climbers, make it comfortable enough for a prolonged watch, and you'll be rewarded beyond your wildest dreams!

You don't have to take such extreme measures to make a hobby of bird watching, of course, although there are several things you can do to encourage a greater variety of birds to visit your garden. First, you can grow plants that attract particular birds – like

Wildflowers for a meadow
Wildlife expert Chris Baines, in his excellent book *The Wild Side of Town*, recommends the following spring-flowering varieties to get your patch of meadow off to a flying start. Packet seed of each is readily available, as are pre-packed meadow flower mixtures. You may even be able to obtain young plants. Never, never, be tempted to take wildflowers from the wild!
● Daisy ● Catsear ● Cowslip ● Bugle ● Selfheal ● Speedwell ● Lesser stitchwort● Fritillary ● Meadow saxifrage ● Yellow rattle ● Lady's smock

sunflowers for greenfinches, berrying subjects for blackbirds and thrushes, teasels for goldfinches. Then, with the aid of a bird-table and various feeding devices, you can provide food that will be appreciated by specific species – for example, cooked scraps or lard/suet for robins, tits and wrens, rotten apples for thrushes, nuts in shells for great spotted woodpeckers and nuthatches. A good pet shop will advise you. Most important, though, is to feed birds only in the winter months, stopping by the breeding season in early spring, and to provide food on a daily basis, not just when you care to remember – the birds will come to rely on you.

The best place for a bird-table is close to the house as it will allow you to view the birds from a nearby window and it will make the provision of food on a regular basis more convenient. So site it near the edge of the lawn, preferably unobscured yet quite near a tree or bush. Put the food out first thing in the morning – catering for birds that like to feed at ground level, too – and remove any that is not eaten after a day or two. A bird bath, of course, would be an added delight.

And while the birds are coming and going, you might well look to the skies as you follow their flight. And here you will find the inspiration for yet another all-consuming pastime, although you would be well advised to wait until nightfall. Astronomy is perhaps the ultimate form of nature watching and you don't have to invest in vast quantities of astronomically expensive gear in order to enjoy it. Why not create a permanent space-age viewing platform as a central feature of your lawn? Build a plinth for your telescope and even devise a revolving seat!

RELAXATION AND ENTERTAINMENT

How many times have friends popped over on a hot summer's day only to find your lawn strewn with a hastily gathered hotchpotch of garden chairs, picnic tables and car rugs? A teacup or two nestles charmingly in the turf and something resembling a barbecue fills the air with that oh so delightful fragrance of firelighters. Own up, it's an all too familiar picture!

Come the warmer weather, we rush outside to catch a few rays or eat alfresco, apparently quite willing to compromise on comfort and sacrifice social graces. We use our garden as an outdoor room but we pay virtually no attention to furnishings, fixtures and fittings. Stepping from the living room onto the lawn is like moving from a mansion into a mobile home!

It would be a shame to use our unpredictable summers as an excuse for not making the most of outdoor living. By taking the trouble to create a tailor-made environment for entertaining and relaxing, not only will you be instantly rewarded on those most perfect of days but you'll be hard pressed to stay indoors, even under threat of rain.

Think of your lawn as a newly laid wall-to-wall carpet. It's an empty room just begging to have seating arranged here, a sunbathing area there. There might be a sheltered alcove in need of a table or two, trees crying out for a hammock. Consider your lifestyle and plan accordingly. Everyone's requirements are different and these, along with the shape, size and aspect of your lawn, will obviously determine which features you include and where you choose to site them.

For example, revellers could turn that central area into a dance floor and have the all-important bar and barbecue in a corner close-by. They would probably want to lay on electricity, too, for music and lighting. Those of a less gregarious disposition on the other hand, shuddering at the thought, could opt for tea for two in a restful retreat and leave the lawn completely clear for quiet contemplation or a game of croquet. Similarly, the planning and placing of features if you are a sun worshipper will revolve solely around the UV rays – maybe having more than one permanent sunbathing area, say. For others, though, a top priority might be to escape the heat of the day under a shady pergola or arbour.

But the lawn needn't be seen as just one room. By using walls, fences and screens as dividers and partitions, you can create different areas, each with their own distinct character and purpose. You can enjoy one or another as the mood takes you or as the occasion demands. And this, of course, is particularly useful where there are children as well as adults to satisfy – youngsters can have their adventure swings, teenagers can have their den and adults can have their well-deserved sanctuary!

Facts of Lawn Life

According to a recent MORI survey, two out of every five lawn owners interviewed never ate in the garden or had barbecues! Of those who did, twice as many ate al fresco with family and friends as with the family alone. A rather sad three percent barbecued or ate outside with friends only!
The most common leisure activity mentioned was sunbathing (46%), followed by sleeping/relaxing (36%), eating/drinking (27%), and reading/writing (10%).

The ultimate in luxury and sophistication is a superb gazebo furnished for maximum comfort and relaxation – a summer retreat that would do any lawn proud

Positioned for best effect, just a single item of garden furniture can stand alone as an intriguing and charming focal point – and the more original it is, of course, the better

Opting for permanent features for relaxation and entertaining also gives you the opportunity to choose tables, chairs, barbecues and so on that will create an harmonious effect while, at the same time, reflecting a particular mood. Strategically placed, they will become an integral part of the overall structure of your garden and, as such, they will belong.

If you fancy giving alfresco dinner parties on a regular basis, for example, then having permanent tables and seating will be imperative. After all, there will be enough to carry to and fro without adding furniture to the list. And, for the same reason, you will want to choose a site that is within relatively easy reach of the kitchen but not, ideally, by the back door in full view of the cooker. The answer here would be to create an outdoor dining room, conveniently close, and use screens smothered in scented climbers to disguise any undesirable views.

Another factor to take into account when deciding where to position sitting areas is noise. Sunbathing, for instance, doesn't demand a great deal of concentration and it also tends to be a somewhat solitary pursuit. A bit of noise, therefore, is unlikely to be a problem – it certainly isn't going to interfere with the tan. A relaxing read, though, or a pleasant afternoon chat over tea and biscuits demands peace and quiet, and that's when you need to be as far away as possible from traffic or noisy neighbours. If lack of space makes that impossible, grow a good thick hedge instead.

Most sedentary activities also require a sheltered site because even in the height of summer the windchill factor can be considerable. Ornamental hedges, screens, walls and fences, as well as providing privacy – and to a greater or lesser extent noise reduction – can all be used to advantage as windbreaks. Make the most of them and you'll spend far more time basking in your bathers than cringing in your cardi!

You don't have to compromise on style for the sake of practicality. A gleaming timber picnic bench unit is great for family meals al fresco and its attractive, solid design gives it a permanence that is fairly unique amongst lower-priced garden furniture

If the garden furniture is stunning enough in its own right – like this intricately woven high-tech range – it is better left to stand alone so that it can be seen in splendid isolation

Keep it Clean

You can get tailor-made protective covers that will fit most standard designs of garden furniture. Made from a heavy-duty, waterproof material, they are coloured green to blend with the lawn and look unobtrusive. The covers are widely available from garden centres and stockists of garden furniture. Many furniture manufacturers offer their own range of covers.

Unless rain is threatening, however, it's unlikely you'll be putting covers on every night or whenever the furniture's not in use – and, in any case, even though they're relatively inconspicuous, they're hardly attractive. Covers or not, regular maintenance and cleaning will help to protect furniture from the elements, keep it looking fresh and prolong its life.

Much ready-made timber furniture is pre-treated and guaranteed against rot, but if it isn't it must be painted with a good wood preservative. Coated timber is also designed to last for years without any treatment, although it will need regular sponging down with a proprietary cleaner. Stone or concrete that gets just a bit too weathered for your liking can be scrubbed with a patio cleaner – these are readily available – while metal furniture can be given a completely new lease of life if necessary with a coat of suitable paint. Any hinges and moving parts must be regularly oiled and all furniture must be thoroughly dried-down if it is to be stored away.

Furniture, cushions and comfort

There is some superb garden furniture around these days – sleek white resin, chunky timber, contemporary, traditional, exhorbitant, dead cheap. Whatever your taste, requirements and budget, you will find something to fit the bill. But the most common mistake people make is to look at furniture in isolation, with little regard as to how it will relate to other features in the garden. For however stylish it might look in that Mediterranean setting in the advert, there's a good chance it will look totally incongruous in your somewhat more humble surroundings, especially if it is simply plonked on the lawn!

The placing of garden furniture, in fact, is often far more important than how it looks. A garden seat as a focal point in the corner of a lawn, perhaps partly hidden from view, will have an intriguing effect whether it's made from wrought iron or rotten wood. A simple bench in a shady arbour will prove irresistible whether it's hewn from stone or built of brick. A grouping of chairs under the shade of a tree will always be inviting, however crude or rustic they might be.

That's not to say, though, that we should return to the days when garden furniture meant a few folding picnic chairs in garish vinyls with a faded deckchair thrown in for good measure! What we should strive for, ideally, is furniture that looks good, serves a purpose and enhances the garden. There are no rules of thumb but if you can meet those three criteria you're on to a winner.

There are two options open to you – to buy ready-made furniture or to construct your own. The latter will invariably work out a lot cheaper and will give you the opportunity to come up with designs that are totally original and tailored to your exact requirements. You might not be able to emulate the work of master craftsmen but the individuality of your furniture will more than make up for any lack of sophistication. That doesn't mean you have to say goodbye to originality if you buy off the peg, of course, but you might have to go further than your local garden centre if you want to find something a bit different. Look at the gardening magazines to see what is available and send off for brochures – as many as possible – before buying.

Off the peg

To create a really convincing permanent feature of outdoor furniture it is better to turn to the more robust materials like wood, stone and cast iron, all of which have an enduring quality and, as such, will grow old gracefully. Lightweight tubular metal tables and chairs, as well as the cheaper plastic ranges, will always appear to be of a flimsy, temporary nature – even though many are perfectly durable – and will rarely integrate well with the rest of the garden. Top of the range plastic or resin furniture is worth considering, however, as it looks as solid and stylish as the very best timber designs.

You might think that this is beginning to sound a rather expensive exercise and, indeed, it can be. Off the peg furniture that is well made, attractive and durable doesn't come cheaply. One way of cutting the cost, though, as long as you're willing to do a bit of work yourself, is to go for kit-form timber furniture that you assemble yourself. Often the wood is pre-treated but if it isn't, which makes it even cheaper, you are almost better off because you can then choose an attractive, coloured preservative-cum-woodstain to give the furniture a really individual finish.

Another reason for choosing robust furniture is stability. And for young children and the elderly it is particularly important to avoid designs that might topple or, in the case of folding tables and chairs, collapse. Again, it's a question of purpose. For family meals and entertaining, you'll want furniture that is solid, with upright chairs at a convenient height and, preferably, an easy to clean, smooth-topped table. For a five-minute break between chores, you can pay less attention to practicalities and concentrate on placing the furniture in a restful setting. For a well-earned afternoon snooze you'll want to go for comfort first and foremost.

Of course there's far more to garden furniture than tables and chairs, although even these supposedly basic items are now available in every imaginable shape and form. Also on offer are hammocks – either on free-standing frames or for hanging between trees – multi-position loungers, swinging sofas, trolleys, footstools, parasols and drinks cabinets. And there are more traditional items, too, like ornate stone benches, carved timber pews and intricate wrought-iron seats. Furniture manufacturers are certainly doing their bit to encourage outdoor living – it simply remains for us to make the most of it!

Home grown
Come up with your own furniture ideas and the sky's the limit – literally, that is, if you fancy a high-rise sunbathing platform! Just use your imagination, throw in a bit of DIY expertise, and before you know it you'll have all the neighbours drooling from their deckchairs. There's no need to be bound by convention, no need to even try and emulate that sunbed in the local showroom.

Perhaps the greatest advantage of making furniture from scratch is that you can tailor it to your exact requirements and make it a perfect fit for your garden – just like a space-saving fitted kitchen with everything neatly and conveniently slotted into place. What's more, you can take heart from the fact that the very simplest of features are often the most effective.

On that note, bear in mind that you can combine different materials to create interesting contrasts in texture. And, by making use of wood stains and paints designed for metal and concrete, you can conjure up any colour scheme under the sun.

On the bench
One of the easiest ways to provide seating is with benches. You could have two stark white concrete plinths supporting planks of gleaming pine, for example; or you could contrast a base of rich russet bricks with an upper surface of cool grey paving slabs. If the brick base were made as a hollow box, you could give it a hinged timber lid-cum-seat and have a handy storage area inside.

A bench on its own could be strategically placed as a focal point – to be seen through an archway, say – while two or three benches could be arranged at right angles to each other as a corner unit. It would be particularly effective, too, if you could arrange the

Protect and Colour the Wood
There is a seemingly overwhelming range of preservatives and wood treatments on the market but basically they are all designed to do the same job – that is, repel water, resist damaging ultraviolet rays, protect from fungal decay and insect attack and, very often, stain the wood. However, you can either opt for a shade that matches the original timber or you can go for a more dramatic effect, which these days could be any colour of the rainbow. Modern-day wood preservatives-cum-stains are largely water based, making application and cleaning of brushes simplicity itself. They are also relatively odourless and, once applied and dry (which takes a matter of hours), are harmless to pets and plants. Prior to application, experiment with the stain on a spare piece of the timber or on a hidden part of the structure. The quality and colour of the original wood – along with the method of application and the number of coats – will have a marked effect on the final result.

Having a substantial tree in your garden may be regarded as a mixed blessing but if you have taken the necessary steps to cope with the shade it casts on the lawn, you can relax and enjoy it. A tree seat will always be inviting, if not irresistible – make one yourself, using a simple bench structure, or buy one in kit-form that needs only to be slotted together

benches in such a way that they follow the exact angles or contours of the lawn – setting them within a semi-circular recess, for instance – or design them so that they reflect the shape of other structures within the garden, like a path, pergola or pool. (This is worth bearing in mind when planning any permanent features, of course, as it will help you to create that all-important element of harmony.)

If you are lucky enough to have a mature tree on your lawn, then why not build a slatted wood bench to encircle its trunk. Seating units designed to do just this, incidentally, can be bought in kit form, ready for you to assemble. Alternatively, you could build a table around the trunk, maybe hexagonal in shape, and surround this with matching benches.

On this note, it hardly needs to be said that the design of your bench can be scaled-up to make a dining table to match or scaled down to make a series of occasional tables – these could be positioned at each end of the bench or in the corner of a right-angled unit. And, finally, for extra comfort you could always put backrests on the benches and add a few cushions.

Retaining walls or brick-raised beds provide the perfect opportunity for incorporating an original and permanent bench seat. Its contours and dimensions can be tailored to your exact requirements and the materials can be chosen to complement those used elsewhere – say, in a path, lawn edging or boundary wall

You may be considering planting some ornamental hedging in the garden, either to border your lawn or to create divisions within it. If this is the case, why not use the opportunity to include some intriguing 'floating' seats? Simply construct a few slatted wood benches, supported by stout timber posts, and position these so that the hedging plants – yew or box would be best – grow up and around the structure. Once the foliage has become level with the seat, and adequately camouflaged the supports, all you have to do is keep the top and sides neatly clipped.

Walling within, or adjacent to, the lawn provides yet another ideal opportunity for creating imaginative seating ideas. Timber, concrete and brick can all be pressed into action and used to form benches that mould themselves exactly to specific contours or angles. They can sit within the wall itself or they can extend outwards, maybe at right angles, into the lawn. A table could be shaped to fit, too, or you could simply incorporate a few shelves into the brickwork so that you have somewhere to put the odd glass, teacup or plate of sandwiches.

In the sun

You won't catch serious sunbathers doubled up in a deckchair. They want to be flat out and free to turn over and fry that other side. Nor will they appreciate people milling around, casting shadows and stumbling over the bottle of sun oil. So, to be fair to them, the sunniest spot on your lawn should be designated a sunbathing-only zone. That done, you can go to town on creating some purpose-built furniture that will be ready for use the minute the sun deigns to make an appearance.

One of the most effective ways of doing this is to build a slatted wood sunbathing deck, supported just a few inches off the ground. The timber frame could be removed for mowing or, alternatively, the grass underneath could be replaced with an area of gravel or paving. You can make the platform any size you like – the dimensions of a single or double bed, for example – but they must be long enough and wide enough to accommodate the average splayed-out bod. And if space allows, of course, you could build several decks and arrange them in an attractive, sociable grouping. Ring the changes, too, by placing the slats, say, diagonally on one frame, vertically on another, and stain and varnish the wood for a

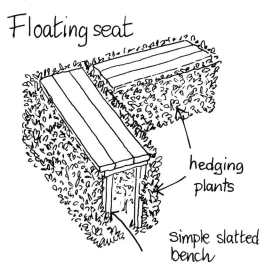

Floating seat

hedging plants

Simple slatted bench

A fun and novel way to combine seating and hedging. A series of 'floating' benches can be established relatively quickly and could be used as effective dividers within the lawn, to separate visually one area from another

gleaming contrast against the grass. Finish off with a collection of cool-coloured cushions.

A variation on the same theme would be to incorporate a hinged section at one end of the deck so that you can create an adjustable backrest. To support the flap, use a deckchair-type bar slotted into notches on the base.

If you're not averse to a little excavation work, then how much more luxurious can you get than to have a sunken sun-trap. A depth of just a foot would be enough to give some added shelter but, obviously, the deeper, the better. Create a pit with gently sloping sides – it can be any shape you like – and then lay turf or sow grass seed over the area. In the base you could insert a timber deck, as described above, or for a real sunbathing treat you could dispense with the grass and plant instead a spongy, aromatic mattress of chamomile.

A similar feature, if you have a sloping site, could be incorporated into a grass bank or terrace. Cut a platform into the slope, so making a wedge-shaped excavation, and retain the earth on the two sides and back with bricks or stout timber planks. Alternatively, you could give the recess gently sloping sides and turf the whole area. The base, once again, could be timber or chamomile, or it could be left as grass.

Something soft

A good deal of shop-bought furniture comes with detachable cushions. In fact, it is often the beautifully subtle or striking designs in upholstery that will make the sale rather than the more practical details of construction and so on. There are styles and patterns to suit every taste – from graphic geometrics to flouncy florals – and there is a seemingly endless supply of co-ordinated accessories.

No-one would argue that the upholstery does a great deal to enhance the furniture, both in terms of comfort and aesthetic appeal. And the matching place mats or parasol certainly help to achieve an attractive, harmonious effect. There is a tendency, though, to rely too heavily on the fabrics so that they alone end up dictating a particular mood, maybe overwhelmingly so. By all means go for those sizzling stripes or palest of polka dots but only

If you have a sloping plot, where the lawn will have to be terraced anyway, then consider creating an ingenious, sheltered sunbathing platform within a grassy bank – the same idea could be used to provide seating, too

if they are going to make a worthwhile contribution to the essential character of the garden. Remember, too, that the more dominant the design, the sooner you are likely to tire of it.

The materials used for outdoor upholstery are water-resistant and fade-resistant – some more so than others – and you could, in theory, leave cushions in place during the summer months. To prolong their life, though, and keep them looking fresh, it would be better to take them in when bad weather threatens. You can buy cushions separately, too, from specialist manufacturers. These come in a host of shapes, styles and sizes – to fit most standard designs of garden chairs and sunloungers – and so, if need be, you can give old furniture a complete face lift at a fraction of the cost of buying new. You can also use them to add a professional touch to DIY furniture, of course, or to simply take the chill off that charming but cold stone seat.

If you're handy with a needle and thread you could make your own cushions, which might be particularly useful if you are designing a chair, seating unit or sunbathing deck that is somewhat different from the norm. All you need to do is get blocks of medium density foam cut to the appropriate size and invest in some heavy duty canvas – this is available from most good upholstery or furnishing stores in an impressive range of colours and patterns. Leave an opening on one side of the cover, fastening it with a zip or Velcro, so that it can be removed for cleaning. And, if you like, treat the canvas with a water-proofing agent for added durability and easy maintenance.

Making your own cushions opens up all sorts of possibilities, of course. As an alternative to conventional garden furniture – especially for children, parties and sunbathing – you could concoct a whole collection of brightly coloured scatter cushions, mattresses and giant bean bags. Or, particularly with youngsters in mind, you could make cushions shaped as cubes, cylinders and oblongs to double as seating units – strips of Velcro will fasten them together – and giant, spongy building bricks.

Barbecues and eating out

You might still find an uninitiated few who insist on using that old grill pan or biscuit tin, balanced precariously on a pile of bricks, to build a makeshift barbecue. But thankfully most homes these days boast at least a basic hibachi and we pride ourselves in being able to burn bangers and burgers to perfection. The 'barbie' has arrived and it's here to stay.

You would probably barbecue even more often, though, if all the necessary paraphernalia were immediately to hand – the equipment permanently set up, the accessories at your fingertips. And so, just like furniture, it makes sense to plan for barbecues and give them a special place on your lawn. It needn't cost a great deal of money and, once done, it will allow you to eat alfresco at the drop of a hat, even in the drizzle.

The barbecues themselves can be as simple or sophisticated as you like. In fact, as long as you are cooking over charcoal, the chances are that the food will taste equally delicious, whether you're using a barbecue picked up for a fiver at the local garage or one with all the latest specifications setting you back up to five

Cooking Tips
Ideally, barbecues should be in a sheltered position but with enough of a draught to keep the charcoal burning. If you use firelighters to get the charcoal alight, wait until they've completely burned out before attempting to cook. Otherwise the fumes will taint the food. The charcoal, when ready, will be glowing pink by night, looking white by day. How quickly the food cooks will depend on the height of the grills, of course, but the nearer they are to the charcoal, the more the fat will hit the fire. It's a good idea, therefore, to have a hand-sprayer of water at the ready so that you can douse any flames with a quick squirt. And, to give your barbecued food that extra special smoky flavour, why not buy a packet of aromatic wood chips to sprinkle amongst the charcoal. Mmmm . . .

There's no shortage of fancy sunloungers in the shops but you could make your own at a fraction of the price and have a far more original feature to set off your hard-earned tan

Give barbecueing a permanent place on the lawn and you can be out there eating al fresco at the drop of a hat. With a tailor-made unit you can have practical work surfaces, built-in shelves and even cupboards and benches – everything can be conveniently to hand, just like in a dream kitchen

hundred pounds. What you should be looking for, though, is convenience, which means different things to different people.

The cordon bleu cook choosing to transfer his or her culinary expertise from the kitchen cooker to the barbecue will probably be in dire need of a model with all mod cons – automatic ignition, separate burners with temperature controls, rotisseries, hoods for roasting – and every imaginable accessory. Food can then be cooked to absolute perfection, as if it had come from the kitchen, and the menu needn't be restricted to those ubiquitous bangers and burgers. What's more, the cook is likely to emerge cool, calm and unruffled.

Here you are talking about top of the range gas-fired barbecues, which come in various degrees of sophistication. They are usually mounted on a trolley, with a shelf to support the butane cylinder, and instead of charcoal they use lava rock, which stays permanently in the firebowl. You still get a charcoal-type flavour to the food but it's fairly tame and almost clinically clean. For some, it's the only way to barbecue.

For many others, though, barbecueing wouldn't be the same without firelighter fumes, streaming eyes and the occasional incinerated specimen ('was *that* a sausage?'). Here, convenience has more to do with size and space – the more of those bangers and burgers, not to mention cooks, the better – a comfortable working height for tending the food and instant access. Barbies will be impromptu affairs, not invitation-only dinner parties.

This is when you want a functional charcoal barbecue, with relatively few frills, which will simply meet your basic requirements. And there are hundreds of different designs on offer, many even with rotisseries, hoods, wheels and shelves. For example, you can get something quite sophisticated and robust, capable of coping with fifty burgers at a time, for well under two hundred pounds. At the opposite end of the price scale, you could have a party grill for dinner *à deux* at under £20.

hibachi

kettle

party grill

BASIC BARBECUE TYPES

Basic charcoal barbecues, being relatively inexpensive, are still the most popular choice – they might not have as many fancy gadgets as gas models, but the flavour of the food is hard to beat

63

Basically, you pay your money and take your choice. But whatever your priorities, bear in mind that the more robust the barbecue, the more durable it will be and the more likely it is to become a permanent feature. An alternative approach, however, would be to opt for a relatively inexpensive and portable hibachi-style barbecue but give it a tailor-made home, built to your exact requirements. That way, you could have a permanent barbecueing area – with convenient work surfaces, shelves and maybe even a cupboard incorporated into the unit – where the hibachi can be set up in seconds.

Units like this can be built from brick or reconstituted decorative stone walling (much cheaper) and can be as simple or elaborate as your DIY skills allow. The structure will need to sit on a fairly solid foundation, though, so it would be best to remove the turf from the immediate vicinity and replace it with a bed of sand topped with paving stones or gravel. Be careful to choose a site that is practical (preferably not under trees) yet where the unit will please the eye and, ideally, choose a brick or stone that will tone with other features in the garden – a path or boundary wall, for example.

You can build exactly this sort of unit and incorporate, if you prefer, a made-to-measure permanent barbecue. And, here, help is at hand from certain barbecue manufacturers who offer all the basic components you will need, such as metal base plates, charcoal grids, wire grills and support strips – even rotisserie kits. There is usually a choice of sizes and styles (some are circular, for example) and their catalogues suggest suitable designs for the brick surround, which you can copy to the letter or make more elaborate, just as long as the crucial internal dimensions remain the same. Assembly instructions are included with the components of course.

It's not recommended that you leave grills and so forth out in all weathers as they will either rust or, at least, begin to look unsightly. Ideally, then, make sure all the components are removable or, alternatively, devise some sort of plastic cover for the barbecue. These are readily available for off the peg models, in a range of styles, specially tailored for a good fit. But while covers like this allow you to keep the barbecue outside for short periods, they will not give adequate protection year-round – certainly take the appliance inside in winter.

There is a host of other accessories, too, all of which are designed to make your barbecue go with a breeze. Fancy fuels and firelighters are guaranteed to get the charcoal smouldering to perfection within minutes – all the sooner with the aid of a pair of wooden bellows or a barbecue fan. And there is every imaginable tool and utensil, from skewers to scrapers, tongs to turners, basting brushes to broilers. Whether you will know what to do with them is another story, of course, but there's absolutely no doubt you'll have lots of fun finding out!

Setting the scene

OK, so you've got the furniture and you've got the food, but what about the icing on the cake – setting a certain mood, creating a hospitable atmosphere? Whether you're throwing a full-scale party or simply having fun with the family, it's worth taking the trouble to do it in style, with conviction. Pay attention to details of decoration, comfort and convenience – even make contingency plans for a change for the worse in the weather – and you can safely say you can do no more. You, too, can relax!

Light fantastic

Features on your lawn that look good by day can be given a whole new dimension when lit at night. And the lighting needn't be something that is turned on only at party time or on the odd summer evening when you happen to be sitting outside. Intriguingly lit views of the garden from inside the house can be exciting and atmospheric all year round, even in the snow!

You will find every imaginable type of garden lighting is at your disposal, from floodlights and lanterns to spotlights and flares. All are generally available from garden centres and DIY superstores, although if you're looking for something a bit different it may be worthwhile contacting specialist manufacturers through the pages of gardening magazines. Remember, too, that many of the companies who make garden furniture and barbecues offer a range of lighting in various styles.

Think carefully about the impression you want to create and use the right light for the job in hand. For a purely ornamental effect – to highlight a statue, say – a discreet spotlight on a spike in the lawn will work admirably. Anything larger might detract the eye and become a focal point in its own right! Around a party or dining area, you want the light to be soft and gentle, and this can be achieved with giant candles or flares (some are even scented) that are stuck directly into the ground. Alternatively, you could hang a lantern or two amidst some nearby climbers or trees so that the light is dramatically diffused.

There are certain places where you will want the light to be purely practical – alongside steps, for example, or immediately above the barbecue. Here the best solution would be to have a really bright but quite small spotlight that can be directed exactly where needed without over-illuminating the surrounding area. The same device can be used to point out danger spots within the lawn – after all, you don't want guests falling into the sandpit or crashing into the swing but, at the same time, you don't necessarily want such features floodlit.

It's far more effective to create several dramatic pockets of light within your lawn – introducing changes of mood here and there – than to rely on just one lamp to illuminate the whole area. In particular, it allows you to focus attention on individual features and invite exploration. For full-scale parties, you could flank an imaginary path with strings of fairy lights, leading guests to a designated spot for, say, dancing or eating. And you could delineate those areas with a combination of streamers and lights strung between posts.

Unless you go for solar-powered lamps, torches or flares, installing garden lighting will necessitate using electricity from your mains supply. By law, cables laid underground must be 18in deep, while a variety of regulations govern the approved height of those carried overhead. Many outdoor lighting systems run on low

Safety Comes First
Be sure to use a circuit breaker with any electrical appliances, be it lighting, hi-fi, a lawnmower or gardening tools. And, preferably, buy modern, low-voltage lighting systems, which are specially designed for garden use. As for installation, play safe and call in a qualified electrician.

Solid timber furniture looks attractive, is stable (an important safety factor) and will last for years. The robust design here is matched by an equally substantial, extra-large parasol

voltage supply, however, which means you simply have to house a transformer in a convenient, weather-proof location and run the cables along an undisturbed route, concealing them with soil or a casing of some description.

For any other sort of electrical installation work, though, it's imperative you employ a qualified electrician. On the same note, while most low voltage garden lights will come complete with a generous length of cable, a transformer and the necessary fittings, it's vitally important you double check the instructions and ensure you have all the necessary components – seek assistance if in doubt.

Against the elements

Our unpredictable climate has made us past masters at clearing the decks within seconds and bidding a hasty retreat come the all too inevitable downpour. Usually it signals the abrupt end of an alfresco gathering, leaving everyone cooped up indoors and staring at the odd forgotten paper plate collecting rainwater and getting soggy out on the lawn.

66

But if you were to provide some form of shelter over, say, the barbecue and eating area, guests would at best have some chance of keeping dry and, at worst, be able to make a civilised retreat, knowing they can return to an undiluted drink once the shower is over. The barbecue won't have been extinguished, the food won't have been washed away. The party can continue.

Some barbecues come with a fixed hood, of course, which will at least save the sausages. But to keep off the rain – or the midday sun for that matter – over a sizeable area you really need to invest in an awning. You could devise a makeshift structure, of course, using old tarpaulins, posts and ropes, but the finished result is unlikely to win any awards for elegance. Far better, then, to buy a purpose-built awning that looks attractive, is easy to erect and can be used time and time again.

Most sophisticated are the garden arbours available from certain furniture manufacturers. Made from waterproofed cloth, in various colourways and patterns, the roof and side drapes are fitted over an aluminium frame, which is supported by guide ropes – just like a mini marquee, although in some cases they would fill the average lawn. Equally charming would be a giant parasol and these, too, are readily available. Supported on a solid central base, the main structure is made from gleaming timber, which contrasts superbly with the natural-coloured fabric – a world apart from their humble relations, the sun umbrellas.

Less flamboyant but rather more reasonably priced would be the Dining Canopy, which is generally available from garden centres and hardware superstores. It's manufactured, rather aptly, by a company called Practical Products. Generously sized, the canopy consists of a woven waterproof sheet supported over stakes anchored by guide ropes. A quick rearrangement of the structure will turn it into a wind shelter, giving protection on one side but reducing the overhead area by half.

As has already been mentioned elsewhere, a good deal of shelter from wind can be achieved with decorative screens. Similarly, overhead protection from rain is possible by fixing panels of transparent plastic between the struts of a pergola. And once the structure is smothered with climbing plants you won't even know they are there – until the next downpour, that is.

It pays to have at least some form of temporary shelter or canopy over the barbecue/eating area – that way, the party can continue even if the fine weather doesn't

MAKING A LAWN

Utility Lawn Grasses

The following grasses are commonly found in seed mixtures to give a hard-wearing surface.

Smooth-stalked meadow grass: Thrives in sandy, light soils and shady areas.

Rough-stalked meadow grass: Prefers loamy, moist sites.

Wood meadow grass: Thrives under shade and in damp areas.

Annual meadow grass: Good under trees. Likes all soil types.

Perennial ryegrass: Prefers moist, fertile soil.

Crested dog's tail: Good on most soils, including chalk.

Timothy: Best in heavy, wet soils.

Lesser Timothy: Finer than Timothy.

Which grass mixture?

There's an amazing 10,000 or so grass species around the world but, fortunately for us, the ones that are commonly used to create a domestic lawn amount to just about a dozen. And choosing is made even easier because these fall into four main types, each with particular characteristics. The finest grasses of all are the fescues, which are used to create a high quality, ornamental lawn. These won't stand up to any rough and tumble. Next in line are the bent grasses, which although fine-leaved are reasonably durable. More hard wearing still are the meadow grasses, while for ultimate durability there are the rye grasses.

For lawns that are going to come in for a good deal of punishment – and if you are to make the most of them they surely will! – the turf will need to be as strong as possible. However, you may feel you can reach a reasonable compromise by opting for a variety of, say, dwarf perennial rye grass (there are some much improved varieties these days) mixed with one of the finer grasses to improve its appearance. This is the most common solution for a utility lawn.

Apart from the obvious advantage of choosing a suitably durable mixture for your lawn – that is having a robust and healthy sward in spite of constant foot traffic and so on – there will be other benefits too. Utility lawn mixtures are far more forgiving in terms of lawn care, being able to take a degree of neglect without coming to undue harm, and are a lot less demanding when it comes to mowing technique. That's not to say you can abandon them completely, though, and you'll certainly be kept busy with the lawn mower come spring and summer – utility grasses are far more rampant than the finer ones.

Hard-wearing grass mixtures are readily available, both in seed form and turf. They are a good deal cheaper than ornamental grasses and, what's more, you can look forward to them getting established really quickly.

It's also worth remembering that some of the utility grasses are particularly well suited to problem areas – for example, where there is shade or where the soil is especially wet and heavy or dry and light. Assess your site carefully, then, before choosing a mixture, as you may find you have to use more than one. And you might even have enough space, of course, to be able to incorporate an ornamental lawn as well as a utility one!

To sow or to turf?

It's a good idea to consider the relative pros and cons of sowing and turfing very carefully. After all, it is hopefully a task that you will only have to carry out once in any garden and so it pays to give it due attention and get it right. The fact that it will be a one-off outlay in financial terms is also worth taking into account – going for the cheapest option now might prove a mistake in the long term.

There's no doubt that seeding a lawn is much cheaper than turfing and the job itself is far easier, involving no heavy loads or lifting, etc. What's more, you can choose to sow your lawn more or less at your leisure, waiting for a good day when the conditions are just right, and so on.

Seeding allows greater flexibility when it comes to selecting grass varieties that will meet your requirements, although specialist turf suppliers are now offering certain specified grass seeds. A more expensive option still would be to go for seeded turf, which is a relatively new product. Here, specific varieties are grown on turf in 1sq yd or 3sq yd pieces, which can be laid very easily, just like a carpet. And, believe it or not, it can be cut and trimmed with a pair of scissors. For a utility lawn, however, the quality of the turf isn't so critical, although it should obviously be weed-free and healthy.

With turf, of course, you can look forward to having what, in effect, is an instant lawn – at least, it will look that way. The truth is that turf takes a few weeks to settle down before being used for normal activity, while seed requires nine to twelve months to establish itself successfully. It may be that you can afford to wait that long before using your lawn to the full and, if so, the advantages of cost and effort might be enough to make you go for seed. But apart from turf being ready for use almost immediately, it also requires far less critical ground preparation than seeding and it can be laid at any time from autumn through winter as long as conditions are reasonably fine. The only drawback, here, is once the turf is delivered you have little choice but to get on with the job – it can't be left stacked up just because it's raining.

The one remaining advantage of turf over seed is that there is no danger of waking up to find your supposed new lawn destroyed by birds and cats, or infested with weeds and diseases. These, it is said, are just a few of the risks involved in seeding but, seemingly against all the odds, vast numbers of superb lawns are nevertheless created from seed every year. In other words, the choice is down to you.

Preparing the ground
Any major ground work that might be required (see 'Planning a Lawn') should be carried out well in advance of the final preparations. Ideally, the ground should be allowed to settle for at least three months and that means doing the work in early summer, ready for sowing or turfing in the autumn. Second best would be to carry out initial preparation in the autumn so that you can sow or turf the following spring. While the land is lying fallow you must hoe it regularly to remove any weeds that might appear. This is particularly important if you are to be sowing seed.

By the time you are ready to sow or turf, the area you have allocated for lawn should be quite level and free of any rubble, plant debris, large stones or clods of earth. And you would also be well advised to apply a balanced fertiliser to the soil about a

While sowing seed and turfing are essentially relatively simple tasks, a degree of diligence and a methodical approach is necessary if the job is to be done successfully. Most important when sowing is to divide the area into measured sections so that the seed can be applied evenly and at the correct rate. When turfing, it's a good idea to work from a plank of wood to protect the grass. Position each turf so that it butts up to its neighbours and check the surface for any bumps and hollows as you proceed – use a spirit level if necessary

week beforehand. You should also have marked out the desired shape of your lawn, using string and pegs for straight edges, a line of sand or a furrow for curves. All you have to do now (when the ground is reasonably dry) is firm the site and produce a friable surface by alternately treading over the earth, digging down with your heels, and raking. Repeat the process several times until your heels leave only a slight depression and the soil is nice and crumbly on top.

How to sow seed

No matter which type of grass mixture you are using it must be sown evenly at a rate of 1–2oz per square yard. This is best achieved by dividing the area into yard square sections, using string and pegs, and sowing the correct weight in each. Make sure the earth is nicely furrowed (the raking should have done this) and sow half the seed in one direction, half in the other. Cover the seed by lightly raking over the surface. Once the area is sown, set up efficient bird-scarers or criss-cross the whole area with black cotton stretched between sticks.

Aftercare

Don't let the mower anywhere near the lawn until the growth is around 3in high. The first cut should trim off only about 1in but after that you can start to mow on a regular basis, gradually reducing the height to about 1in. Whatever quality of grass you are using, certainly don't mow shorter than ½in in the first year. Even if weeds were treated prior to sowing, it's inevitable more will spring up with the new grass. If these can't be dealt with by hand, use a selective weedkiller once you have mown the lawn about half a dozen times. Watering is only necessary if conditions are particularly dry and then it must be done copiously and frequently. Look out for any signs of disease and treat accordingly. Wait six months before applying a lawn fertiliser to your lawn and preferably nine to twelve months before using it for recreation and leisure activities.

How to lay turf

You can get off to the best possible start by finding a specialist supplier who will provide you with the lawn grasses of your choice rather than 'just any old turf'. That done, you can set about the relatively simple task of laying the turves in a brickwork pattern (that is, staggering the joins) over the prepared ground. Don't worry about trying to get them to fit your exact lawn shape – instead, just let them overhang the edges where necessary and keep the final trimming right to the end. Once all the turves have been laid, brush a quantity of sifted compost into the joints (to encourage them to knit together) and, to the same end, go over the area with a roller (if the turf is dry) or a tamping tool. If there are bumps, flatten the ground underneath (rather than trying to bash the turf down!) and if there are any obvious bare patches, sow them with a mixture of compost and grass seed (see Lawncare Calendar on page 78 for appropriate timing).

Aftercare

It might look as if you have an instant lawn but, while you will be able to use it a lot sooner than a seeded one, you must nevertheless keep off it for several weeks in order to let the turf settle down. If you lay the lawn in the autumn this is unlikely to be particularly inconvenient. As with lawns from seed, the first mowing should be quite high, reducing the cut gradually over a period of weeks. Both a fertiliser and top-dressing (see Lawncare Calendar on page 78) can be applied in the spring.

LOOKING AFTER YOUR LAWN

In the Beginning

If it hadn't been for the invention of the mower in the early part of the nineteenth century, the lawn would have remained the sole preserve of rich land owners. Up until then, after all, scything or grazing animals were the only ways of keeping the grass down and few ordinary folk had either the time or means to do that. It is Edwin Budding who we have to thank for the advent of the great British lawn. He was a foreman working in a textile factory in Stroud, and he saw how a machine that was being used to trim the pile on cloth could be adapted to cut grass. In 1830 his design for the first cylinder mower was patented and a couple of years later Ransomes went into production with two models, one costing seven guineas, the other costing ten. Sadly, the invention brought Budding no great fortune since he signed away his rights to a share of the profits in his eagerness to see the machine in production. He died in 1840, some say broken-hearted.

Seeing as your lawn is going to give you so much pleasure, it's only fair that you return the favour and look after it. If you don't, the harsh reality is that before long you won't have much of a lawn to enjoy anyway. In the course of a year the turf will have taken a good deal of punishment, being trampled and pounded by feet, knocked and flattened by toys and games, gouged and scuffed by garden furniture. Who would blame it for throwing down its blades and dying?

Fortunately, the grass family includes some fairly tough characters and, as discussed under 'Planning a Lawn', you can do much to save undue wear and tear by choosing a suitably coarse mixture in the first place – that is, if you are starting a lawn from scratch. Those who are stuck with a finer quality of turf will simply have to work doubly hard to keep it in shape.

Whatever type of grass you have, though, it is vital you look beneath the surface and pay attention to the inner health of your lawn. Grass is no different from any other plant, after all, and requires equally good soil, adequate moisture and a supply of food. But because a lawn is made up of so many thousands of tiny plants, all crammed together, tending to their needs demands a completely different approach to cultivation, using a range of special techniques. Let's start with the equipment you'll need . . .

What you need

The least popular gardening activity, according to a national survey, is weeding. Mowing, surprise, surprise, comes close on its heels in second place! If you have a lawn you will obviously need to invest in a mower and, judging from general opinion, you will want one that does the job as quickly and efficiently as possible. But with such an apparently vast range of different models on the market, making the right choice does require a basic understanding of the different types – wheeled rotary, hover or cylinder – and what they can or can't do. And if you want to make really light work of mowing you'll also have to choose between electric or petrol-powered machines. The factors that will govern your choice here are quite specific.

It would make sense to look first at the rotary, which accounts for about three-quarters of all current mower sales. Because rotary mowers have blades that rotate horizontally at a very high speed, cutting the grass with a scythe-like action, they can cope particularly well with rough, uneven ground and long grass – even when wet if the blades are sharp. You won't get such a pristine finish as with a well-adjusted cylinder mower, but it will be perfectly acceptable for most purposes. And any shortcomings here are anyway far outweighed by the further advantages of easy maintenance (blades are simply replaced, not sharpened) and comparatively low cost.

The hover is also a rotary but, instead of being wheeled, it uses a fan to create an aircushion beneath the mower, making it float above the lawn like a hovercraft. Consequently, hovers make light work of mowing undulating ground and slopes and, what's more, they cut both dry and wet grass equally efficiently.

So, it's easy enough to understand why rotaries, whether wheeled or hover, are the most popular choice. But there is still the question of power to consider, since both electric and petrol-driven rotary mowers are available. First and foremost, electric models are lighter to handle, cleaner and quieter in operation and less expensive. And this is also true of electric cylinders, of course. It's not surprising, then, that the vast majority of mowers sold today run off mains electricity.

But there is one governing factor that has to be taken into account. Electric machines are ideal if the furthest corners of your garden are no more than 200ft from a power point. However, if a cable has to be any longer there is the possibility that the power may fluctuate and cause the machine to overheat. In larger gardens, therefore, you will have to consider a petrol-driven mower and simply offset the disadvantages of greater maintenance, cost and weight against the advantages of independence from an external power source and freedom from trailing cables (see safety guidelines in 'When and how to mow').

Just because the rotary mower is the most popular machine today, it doesn't mean the traditional cylinder-type mower should be dismissed out of hand. The market for them might be on the decline but they still account for about a quarter of all mower sales. The scissor-like action of the blades, as long as they are sharp and properly adjusted, will give the quality of cut imperative for a prize-winning, bowling-green finish. Powered versions fitted with a hefty roller will provide zebra stripes. But considering the disadvantages of expense and increased maintenance – along with the fact that they don't cope well with long or wet grass or uneven ground – the cylinder mower is only worth considering if a lawn is to be mainly ornamental.

It's also worth noting that facilities such as a roller and grass collection – once only available on cylinder mowers – can now be enjoyed on certain rotary models too. Rollers, unless substantial, won't do much to achieve a striped finish, but a grass box will be of enormous help, saving you the extra work of forever clearing clippings in order to keep your lawn looking neat and healthy. Hovers, obviously, don't have rollers.

The final consideration when choosing a mower is size – that is, the size of your lawn in relation to the width of cut of the mower. The wider the cut, the sooner the job will be done, of course, but that doesn't mean you should go so far as to have a massive petrol model in a handkerchief-sized plot. Economically, it wouldn't make sense and, apart from anything else, it would be almost impossible to manoeuvre! The cutting widths of the most popular electric rotaries range from around 10in to 18in, while the petrol-driven models are anything from 14in to 30in. So, choose an appropriate width, taking into account any narrow strips of grass

Awkward Corners
For all those hard to get at places on your lawn – around the barbecue unit, underneath furniture, up against screens and fences – you'll find a nylon line trimmer will come in really handy. Lightweight electric models are extremely easy to handle and, considering the time and effort they save in trying to manipulate the mower or resorting to hand shearing, they are likely to prove a really sound investment. As with all electrical appliances used in the garden, be sure to install a circuit breaker in case of power failure or accident. And when using the nylon line trimmer, always wear gloves, goggles and adequate clothing – flying debris can be lethal.

Weeds, Pests and Diseases

As you will see, a thorough programme of lawncare, followed year in and year out, will do much to reduce any problems with weeds, pests and diseases. And it will also mean there is less likelihood of you having to resort to chemical controls – which must be a good thing. There comes a time in even the best tended gardens, however, when the use of a chemical at some stage is really unavoidable. So be prepared. There are many products on the market, specially formulated to treat particular problems. Their development and manufacture are subject to strict regulations and all the necessary safety factors are taken into account. Ultimately, though, the onus is on you, the user, to read the labels and follow instructions to the letter.

Judging by the seemingly endless lists one finds in gardening books of lawn weeds, pests and diseases – far too many to mention here – it appears remarkable that any lawn could be anything but a disaster area. But take heart. The great British lawn is alive and well and that's basically because grass just loves the British climate!

A pair of long-handled edging shears will prove indispensable for trimming and tidying the grass the mower missed or couldn't reach

or awkward corners you may have to negotiate. And, if you have a particularly large plot, consider a self-propelled lawn mower or even a ride-on.

It probably won't come as any surprise to learn that you could spend a small fortune accumulating all the latest lawncare gadgets, tools and equipment. The best advice at this stage, though, is to invest only in those items that are absolutely necessary in order to maintain your lawn in a healthy and presentable condition. You needn't go for the fanciest or most expensive products but you do want to make sure you have the right tools for the job in hand. That way, the work will be done that much more quickly and you'll have more time to enjoy the fruits of your labours.

The basic tools you will need relate to the routine lawncare tasks detailed over the following pages. Some will be used maybe only a few times a year, others on a regular basis throughout the spring and summer. Bear this in mind and be prepared to spend more on the latter so that you get high quality, durable products. Consider, too, that since the majority of lawncare items are used on a seasonal basis, there's no need to buy everything in one go. Spreading the cost through the year might mean you can go for the best every time.

Lawncare activity is at its height in summer, and after the mower, it will be a lawn sprinkler and edging tools that will be in most frequent use. Sprinklers obviously require hosepipes and there are now ones that are flat when not in use and are wound out from a specially designed reel. They're extremely convenient and easy to handle, and space-saving when it comes to storage. Traditional hoses, which tend to be more durable, can also be kept on a reel, albeit a larger one. The only real drawback with these is that they are generally less manageable, requiring careful draining and coiling up after use. As for sprinklers, you can't go wrong with one of the modern designs that rotate or oscillate, giving superb coverage, often in a variety of patterns – and, what's more, the children will love it!

As mentioned elsewhere, you can create a neat edge by bordering the lawn with, say, bricks, strips of wood or edging stones. And if sunk slightly below the level of the lawn, you can mow right to the edge, minimising the need for trimming and tidying. But if this isn't feasible, you'll need an efficient pair of long-handled edging shears to trim the grass not reached by the mower. You could invest in a mechanical trimmer, of course – especially if you have a large lawn – but you'll still find a need for hand shears to finish off the awkward bits. In the absence of an edging material you'll also have to re-cut the lawn edges from time to time in order to keep the grass healthy and neat. For this you must have a half-moon edging iron, which you use like a spade. To get a straight edge, work against a plank of wood; to achieve a contour, follow a length of flexible hose.

Getting slightly more technical, there comes a time in the lawncare calendar when you have to pay attention to the hidden workings of your lawn – what the eye doesn't see. By the end of the summer your lawn will have taken a good deal of pounding and it will be in dire need of a pick-me-up. This involves letting

air into the surface soil (scarifying) and into the subsoil (aerating), and applying a fertiliser to replenish the soil and encourage healthy growth.

Over a small area, scarifying can be carried out with a spring-tined rake, which is indispensable for gathering up autumn leaves as well as getting rid of that dead moss and thatch. Similarly, for aerating you can use an ordinary garden fork, sinking the tines into the ground at, say, six-inch intervals. To save unnecessary backache, however – especially if you have a medium to large lawn – it may well be worth your while investing in a mechanised scarifier and aerator, of which there are several designs.

Fertiliser needs to be applied strictly according to the instructions on the packet, in a measured dose. That means spreading the mixture evenly and consistently over the whole area. There are various hand-held or wheeled devices available to do the job, although how accurately they spread the fertiliser is still dependent on the diligence of the user – that is, walking at a particular speed. The alternative is a powered fertiliser distributor that applies the correct, measured dose no matter how quickly or slowly you are able to cover the area.

The majority of lawn-owners want to get the job of mowing over and done with as easily and as quickly as possible – hence the popularity of lightweight electric rotary models. This is a Flymo Minimo SX

Scarifying – it's important to keep the lawn healthy by raking out dead grass (thatch) and letting air into the surface

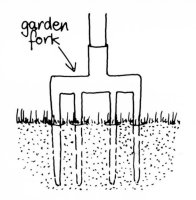

Aerating – use an ordinary garden fork to create air channels at regular intervals across the lawn

Have you met Mr Mole?

Anyone who has woken in the morning to find their wonderful sward littered with tell-tale mounds of earth will not be in the mood to appreciate the more endearing qualities of the mole. The good news, though, if you haven't yet been paid a visit, is that the best deterrent is human activity – the more you use your lawn, the less likely the mole is to take up residence. And you're also in luck if your soil is rather heavy. Moles prefer a light, sandy plot through which to tunnel.

Once moles are in evidence, you will probably have to take quite drastic measures to eradicate them. There are all manner of potions and devices you can try inserting in their runs, from moth balls to proprietary smoke cones to vibrators, but very often it is only trapping or poisoning that is really effective. And, in both these cases, it's vital you seek the help of a professional.

Sweeping – a besom or broom can be pressed into action for sweeping up autumn leaves and scattering wormcasts prior to mowing

You'll be lucky indeed not to have the odd weed finding its way into your lawn, especially if it is a newly created one. The majority are fairly easily dealt with, either by pulling them up by hand, treating them with a special preparation called lawn sand, or, if absolutely necessary, resorting to chemical treatments. A small trowel will suffice for the removal of individual weeds but for the application of the latter you will require either a watering can with dribble bar or a knapsack sprayer with a lance – various models are available. Most important, though, is that the watering can or sprayer is only ever used for the application of weedkiller. Write 'weedkiller' on it in big letters and store it out of the way.

The last remaining essential item is a good old-fashioned besom. Use it to sweep up leaves in autumn, demolish any wormcasts prior to mowing, and keep the lawn free of litter and debris. All of which, of course, can be jobs for the children!

When and how to mow

There's more to mowing than meets the eye and unless carried out properly you'll do your lawn more harm than good. Most important is to maintain the correct height by mowing regularly – generally once a week as soon as the grass is actively growing and maybe more often at the height of the season. The biggest mistake is when people allow the grass to get out of hand and then rush in to give it a crew-cut. Be warned, drastic action like that can cause severe stress and may even kill the grass. Another common misconception is that mowing really short will produce that much sought-after velvety turf. The truth, however, is that the very best lawns are never shorn – they're simply carefully and regularly maintained. For a general purpose utility lawn you should keep the height of the grass (and set the cut of your lawnmower accordingly) at between ½in and 1in during the main growing season. Fine, ornamental lawns should be about half that height. In early spring and autumn the height should be raised by about a quarter of an inch. If for some reason the grass does get over-long – maybe when you are away – start with a high cut and reduce it gradually over a couple of mowings.

Before you start to mow, first check over the machine to make sure it is properly adjusted and so on. And make sure the conditions are right for mowing, of course. While some machines can cope with wet grass, you will get far better results if it is dry. Also, unless you have a hover, make sure the ground itself isn't too wet otherwise the turf could get badly damaged. All that remains then is to scour the lawn for any small objects that could damage the mower or get thrown up and hit somebody – small stones, debris from a party or children's trinkets are the worst offenders – and to scatter any wormcasts with a stiff brush.

Always start by mowing the tricky bits first – usually in the corners and around the edges – and then cover the lawn methodically in straight lines from one end to the other. Use a grass collection box if possible but certainly remove the clippings unless the weather is very hot and dry, in which case they can be left as a mulch to retain moisture in the soil.

If you have a roller fitted and want to make a feature of the stripes, take particular care to run the mower in a regular pattern and try to complete that last run so that the mower can be returned to the shed or garage without ruining the effect. Ideally, alter the direction of the stripes from time to time to avoid ridging.

As for safety, here are just a few words of warning. Don't mow the grass in bare feet or sandals – always wear a stout pair of shoes – and don't fiddle with a mower when the power is on. If adjustments need to be made, first remove the plug cap (petrol) or plug from socket (electric). With electric mowers, keep the cable clear of the machine and always start mowing on the side of the lawn nearest to the power point – that way, there will be no risk of running over the cable. Remember, finally, that mowing the lawn is one game all the family cannot play, so keep children and pets well away.

Top dressing – use the back of a rake to work compost into the air channels created by aerating

Why and when to feed

All plants take nourishment from the soil and grass is no exception. In order to maintain healthy growth, the main nutrients that need to be replenished are nitrogen (N), phosphorus (P) and potassium, (K), and these can be applied to your lawn in the form of fertiliser mixtures. You'll find a whole range of such products lining the shelves of garden centres and so forth – some in liquid form, some as granules or powders – and by reading the labels it is easy enough to find one that will meet your requirements.

It may be useful, however, to understand why the fertiliser you apply to your lawn in spring will be different to the one you use in autumn. All lawn fertilisers are made up of the above three nutrients yet in varying proportions, according to the job they have to do. For example, in spring you want to encourage healthy growth of foliage and so the fertiliser will contain extra nitrogen. In autumn, you want to encourage healthy root development and so the fertiliser will be rich in phosphorus.

Fortunately, the manufacturers have got their preparations right, so we don't have to worry too much about N, P, K ratios. What we must do, though, is follow the instructions on the label.

How top-dressing helps

Healthy grass depends on healthy soil and that means you not only have to replenish the nutrients but you must also improve its texture from time to time. Fertiliser mixtures do little to help here and that is why gardeners, and especially greenkeepers, also use the tried and trusted technique of top-dressing with compost. If you haven't got a source of well-rotted garden compost, you can buy ready prepared mixtures from any garden centre or gardening department. Ideally, top-dress in early spring and late autumn so that it doesn't interfere with mowing.

But don't imagine that your beautiful lawn is going to disappear under a blanket of brown matter! Top-dressing involves first aerating the entire surface, using a garden fork or mechanical device (referred to earlier), and then spreading a fine layer of compost in regular strips along and across the lawn, chequerboard fashion. The compost is then worked into the turf, through the air channels you have created, using the back of a rake or a tool that is specially designed for the purpose. After that you simply use a stiff brush to scatter the excess compost around the lawn.

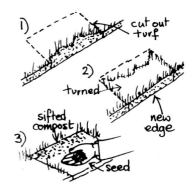

If lawn edges are damaged, it's a relatively simple task to cut and turn the affected area of turf. The bare patch can then be covered with sifted compost and sown with a suitable grass seed – remember to provide protection from birds and cats until the new grass is established

LAWNCARE CALENDAR

Spring (March, April, May)

★ As early as possible, resume regular mowing, remembering to always first check the lawn for small stones, etc and to scatter any wormcasts. Don't make the first few cuts too short – start with the mower set high (around an inch and a quarter) and gradually reduce the height over a period of a few weeks. An ideal height for a utility lawn is from ½in to 1in.

★ If turf was laid in the autumn, winter frost may have lifted it slightly – use a roller, quite lightly, to flatten it down.

★ If you've opted for spring to sow or lay a new lawn, April/May is the ideal time.

★ Early spring is the time to treat moss and weeds. Moss killer should be applied and seen to have worked before doing any raking – that will just make matters worse. Treat actively growing weeds with a selective weedkiller, according to instructions.

★ Wait six weeks after any chemical treatments before attempting to re-seed any damaged or bare patches of lawn.

★ Lightly scarify the lawn surface, removing plant debris and lifting prostrate stems.

★ Aerate the lawn and work in a top-dressing of good garden compost or soil and peat. Brush off the excess.

★ As spring develops and the grass is growing well, apply a nitrogen-rich spring fertiliser to encourage strong top growth.

★ Step up the frequency of cutting as the flowering stage approaches in late spring. Prior to each mowing, use a brush to raise up the flower heads of any annual meadow grass so that they can be cut off and removed along with the clippings.

Summer (June, July, August)

★ Certainly by now, if there are dry spells, you should be ready to water the lawn before it shows any obvious signs of stress. Always water copiously and, during hot weather especially, preferably in the evening. Use as fine a spray as possible.

★ Cut the lawn twice a week. If the weather is dry, raise the cutting height slightly and leave the clippings on the lawn to act as a mulch and conserve moisture in the ground.

★ Trim and tidy lawn edges on a weekly basis.

★ In very hot and dry weather, lightly prick over the lawn surface with a fork or rake before watering.

★ Keep an eye out for weeds and treat accordingly.

★ If you go away on holiday, try to arrange for someone to cut (and if need be, water) the grass. If you can't, raise the cutting height of the mower for the first cut on your return.

★ If the grass needs it, apply a second treatment of nitrogen-rich fertiliser but at half-strength. This must not be used after the month of August.

★ By the end of August you can start sowing seed or laying turf – either to create a new lawn or to carry out repairs. Bear in mind, though, that the need for regular mowing might make large-scale renovations impractical at this time of the year.

Lawncare Calendar

Autumn (September, October, November)

★ Aerate the lawn and apply a phosphorus-rich autumn feed.

★ Raise the height of the cut by a quarter of an inch.

★ As mowing becomes less frequent, top-dress the lawn with good garden compost, peat or leafmould.

★ Clear fallen leaves on a regular basis, putting them into bin-liners (slightly ventilated) or making them into a heap. Leave them to decay and you'll have a ready supply of leafmould.

★ Use a systemic fungicide to treat any lawn diseases.

★ Watch for signs of pest activity, especially chafer grubs and leatherjackets, and use an appropriate pesticide.

★ Treat any moss, as in spring.

★ The surface area of lawns in shade can become sour at this time of year. Aerate the area and apply a dressing of carbonate of lime at a rate of 1–2oz per square yard.

★ Re-sow areas that are badly worn with a more suitable mixture of grass seed – that is, one that is tougher or, if in shade, one that tolerates such conditions.

★ Late September/early October is the ideal time for laying turf.

★ Aim to complete all seed sowing by the end of October.

★ Mowing should all but cease by the end of October too. If you have a hover (to save damage to the invariably damp turf) and the grass is growing because the weather is mild, the occasional trim at a high setting wouldn't go amiss.

★ Clean and maintain all equipment and store away for winter.

Winter (December, January, February)

★ Continue to clear fallen leaves and debris from the lawn.

★ Try to keep off the lawn when it is wet or frosty.

★ Turfing can be carried out in fine weather.

★ An application of fungicide before the snows come will help guard against an attack of Fusarium Patch disease, which is encouraged by the humid conditions that build up under snow.

★ By the end of February, if the conditions are fine, you can prepare the ground ready for any sowing in spring.

★ Overhaul lawncare equipment in readiness for the new season.

★ If wormcasts appear, wait until they are dry and then use a besom to scatter them.

STRUCTURES AND SPECIAL FEATURES

The simplest of archways, placed with care to, say, frame a view or focal point, has instant effect and is especially valuable in a new garden where a structural element has yet to be established

Icing the cake

Every garden benefits from having, in landscape design jargon, a structural backbone. That is, a combination of permanent features, using plantings as well as hard landscaping materials, that work together to make a positive yet harmonious statement. We've already discussed how you can plan your garden to make the best use of your lawn but, meanwhile, we've also suggested numerous ideas for fun playthings, entertainment and relaxation, many of which involve the building or incorporation of structures. The icing on the cake, therefore, in terms of making your garden look attractive, is paying attention to details of construction and striving to achieve a visually pleasing overall effect.

What you don't want is a less than meticulous do-it-yourself enthusiast littering the lawn with a disorderly array of Heath Robinson type affairs, each fighting for attention and ending up an eyesore! What you do want is a series of strategically placed, aesthetically interesting structures, each acting as an attractive focal point yet each with a common theme to provide the vital link. This is where the style, colour and texture of the materials you use become so important.

Where structures are made of timber, it will help if you can use the same wood type throughout. Where this is inappropriate, you can make use of the many modern woodstains available to create an overall colour scheme. The possibilities are endless, with colours ranging from the subtlest of forest greens to rich, glowing reds, and every imaginable shade of natural timber.

Structures can be linked physically, too, by means of pathways, steps, arches, screens and pergolas. Again, avoid a hotch-potch of materials, otherwise the unifying effect will be lost, and stick to a common design theme. This could be anything from the rustic to the high-tech or classical, but, ideally, your chosen style should be in keeping with both the architecture of your house and the general scale of your garden – a grand, Italianate gazebo would look somewhat out of place on the pocket handkerchief lawn of a tiny terraced cottage!

But whether you are building the structures yourself or buying them in, you'll have no trouble finding materials and products to meet your every requirement. The choice is enormous, as you will discover by paying a visit to any major garden centre or by leafing through the pages of any of our leading gardening magazines. Manufacturers of outdoor leisure and landscaping products are coming up with ever more imaginative, high quality ranges, all designed to both enhance our gardens and make our lives that much easier and more enjoyable. Even better news, finding something to fit the bill needn't break the bank.

A place for a path

Unless you have a large expanse of lawn, a path of any description will only serve to interrupt the fun and games. As discussed under 'Planning a Lawn', owners of smaller gardens would be best advised to run a discreet service path – maybe even screened from view – along the perimeter of the garden, leaving as big an area of open lawn as possible. This is certainly the best option if you have young children or plan to play games like croquet, badminton and the like.

But where there's plenty of space, or where the lawn is to be used purely for entertainment and quieter forms of relaxation, there is the opportunity of using paths to provide an interesting and attractive framework, linking the various features you have created and delineating areas allocated to particular activities and so forth. In sizeable gardens, the path can twist and turn, its character changing according to the mood and purpose of the immediate area – a woodland track of chopped bark and sawn log stepping-stones could flank an adventure play area, for example, or a timber walkway could take you to the outdoor gymnasium.

This approach applied to the smaller garden, however, where the whole area can be viewed in one fell swoop, would simply result in a messy jumble of colours and textures. Far better, here, to stick to just one style of path that follows a simple yet attractive route, skirting the most appealing features within your lawn and steering you in a particular direction – to the barbecue, say, or the sunbathing decks.

Perhaps the most practical surface for a path is paving slabs and these come in a host of mellow shades and interesting textures, and also in numerous shapes and sizes, to allow you to create highly individual and attractive arrangements. Brick setts, although rather more expensive, are even more versatile. With all of these, the effect can be softened by spacing the units slightly apart to allow grasses, mosses and seedling wild flowers to spring up in the gaps in between.

Of course you don't have to stick to just one type of paving material. For a clean, contemporary look you could have the smoothest of paving stones edged with brick. Or for a softer,

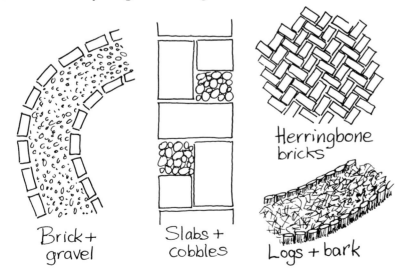

Brick + gravel

Slabs + cobbles

Herringbone bricks

Logs + bark

Choose paving materials with care to reflect a particular mood or style of landscaping or architecture. There's an enormous range at your disposal, each with their own special characteristics – the only limit is your imagination

cottage garden effect you could have gravel flanked by cobbles. Remember to try and choose materials that are in keeping with the architecture of your house and also, ideally, are indigenous to your area. Of course timber can be incorporated, too, and this is particularly effective if it is reflected elsewhere in the garden – the same texture and colour of timber being echoed in, say, garden furniture, trellis and planters. Similarly, bricks can be chosen to match your DIY barbecue, and paving stones or cobbles can be picked up in an edging around the lawn.

The scope is enormous and the one thing you mustn't do is apologise for deciding to include a path within your lawn. Do it with conviction and you'll see that, set against a rich green sward, the effect can be absolutely stunning.

Changing levels

A sloping garden, believe it or not, is the designer's delight and joy. Changes of level, however slight, offer the greatest scope for creating a stunning garden, and landscape architects will very often go to extraordinarily costly lengths to excavate and re-shape a flat-as-a-pancake plot. We've already discussed the necessity, if you are to make any use of your lawn at all, for terracing a sloping garden. Hopefully, by now, the initial shock will have passed and you can begin to look forward to reaping the rewards!

Large sweeping terraces of lawn linked by gentle grassy banks and a few shallow steps would be the ideal, the natural divisions created by each change of level allowing you to site a sunbathing area here, a barbecue unit there. In order to maintain as big an area of terrace as possible in the smaller sloping garden, however, you would probably only be able to accommodate one change of level and it might have to be quite a deep one at that. This is when you have to start thinking about retaining walls, serious flights of steps and some form of walling, hedging or screening to prevent people going over the edge!

But the beauty of a situation like this is that it gives you every

Make easy work of mowing and avoid giving your plants an unexpected haircut by surrounding borders with an attractively staggered arrangement of paving stones – sink them below the level of the lawn so you can mow over the edge

opportunity to let your imagination and creativity run riot. And remember, features that serve a purpose are invariably more convincing than those that are included purely for effect. The screen that divides, say, the upper level where the sandpit is from the barbecue area below – maybe with a pergola overhead – is going to keep the toddlers safe and at the same time look delightful. Similarly, a retaining wall that can incorporate tables and seats – and maybe even the barbecue – is going to look as if it definitely belongs.

The style of steps you choose to incorporate can have a marked effect on the overall design of your garden. Set into a grassy terrace, they can look discreet; projecting outwards, they can look imposing. Built of brick and concrete flags they will appear bold and modern; tumbling out of cobbles and random stone they will seem soft and traditional. Primarily, however, the steps must be practical, which means they must be stable and the riser no more than 6in high, the tread at least 12in deep, preferably 18in. As a rule of thumb, the broader and shallower, the better they'll do justice to both you and your terraced lawn.

Raised beds are a highly practical option in the growing-up garden. Plants are less likely to be disturbed by trampling feet and the surround offers protection from rolling balls

On the edge

Providing some form of edging for your lawn is like putting a picture in a frame. It defines the shape, focuses the eye and enhances that which is contained within. A lawn edging makes a positive statement and, by protecting the grass from wear and tear, gives a neat, professional finish. Even the simplest form of proprietary plastic tape will do much to achieve the desired effect. As, of course, will regular trimming and tidying of the outer fringes of grass missed by the mower.

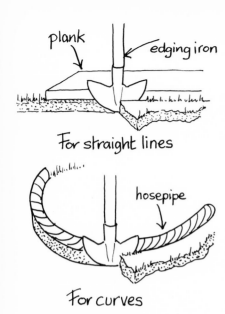

For straight lines

For curves

In the absence of an edging material, keep the lawn in shape with an edging iron – cut against a plank for straight edges, use a garden hose as a template for curves

By sinking edging bricks or paving an inch or so below the level of the lawn, the mower can be taken along the edge for a neat and convenient cut

For easy maintenance

More substantial forms of edging will do all of the above yet also be aesthetically pleasing in their own right. And they give you the opportunity to use materials that will form interesting contrasts of texture, form and colour, ideally providing an effective visual link with the structures or hard landscaping you have created elsewhere within the lawn.

Your choice of lawn edging should be determined by the same factors that were outlined in relation to paths – the need for practicality, the appropriateness of scale and the desirability of particular materials. While a smooth, discreet, concrete edging stone would be ideal in the smaller, modern garden, it might look decidedly out of place in the informal cottage garden. Here, an edge of decorative stone or cobbles would be more appropriate. Similarly, a brick edging would look superb if related to brick-built features elsewhere but would be an unfortunate addition to the rustic or woodland garden. In this case, an edge of timber would be a better choice. There is a wealth of materials that can be put to imaginative use, as well as a host of proprietary products, including more unusual ones like mini logs or faithfully reproduced Victorian clay tiles.

Where the lawn edge borders a flowerbed – and especially if it is irregularly shaped – your could surround it with an attractive, staggered arrangement of paving slabs. Bedded an inch or so below the level of the lawn, they will allow you to mow right to the edge, dispensing with all those complicated manoeuvres and at the same time avoiding the danger of giving your plants an unexpected haircut.

An alternative solution would be to raise flowerbeds above the level of the lawn, retaining the earth with a low stone or brick wall or with hefty timber beams or logs – the latter are available ready-cut and strung together on a roll, making the job extremely easy. Of course, an added advantage of creating raised beds is that the plants are afforded a degree of protection from trampling little feet and rolling croquet or cricket balls!

Arches and arbours and things
Everyone knows what a garden arch is but few are that clear on the definition of arbours, pergolas and gazebos – terms commonly used to describe a variety of garden structures yet very often wrongly applied. The confusion is understandable as the three are closely related and serve a similar purpose. Perhaps, then, it doesn't matter whether you get the terminology right or not, just as long as you know what you want when you see it! For the record, though, a brief description of these garden structures might prove worthwhile.

An arbour is a shady retreat, strictly speaking formed by a bower of trees or climbing plants and primarily used for housing a garden bench or chair. In fact, although now obsolete, any grassy seat was once called an arbour. The simple, dome-shaped structures that are available today – usually made from tubular metal – are designed specifically to support climbing plants and form an arbour. They are of little decorative or practical value in their own right, although a coat of brightly coloured paint to match a garden seat within could transform what is a relatively cheap structure into an instant and highly attractive focal point. But, until it has a cladding of plant material, it wouldn't really be an arbour and it certainly wouldn't be a shady retreat.

The word pergola is derived from the Latin, *pergula*, meaning 'shed', but the structure it is now used to describe bears little resemblance to a garden outhouse. A pergola is where a series of overhead beams are supported by pillars of concrete or stone or by timber posts, originally along a walkway. Again, the structure is designed to be decked with climbing plants and so provide welcome shade and a feeling of intimacy. These days pergolas are more often used to frame a seating area or patio than cover a stretch of path, and as a result they tend to be rectangular in shape rather than oblong. However, most kit-form pergolas are designed on a modular basis and you can create more or less any shape you like. The wood is usually pre-treated and the kits come with all the necessary fixings and instructions. Panels of trellis can be tailored to fit the sides, so making for greater privacy and shelter – ultimately, an outdoor room.

Look up gazebo in the dictionary and you will probably see the definition 'a belvedere' – and you'll be none the wiser! In fact, this is misleading anyway as a belvedere is a building with no walls, usually sited on high ground or even at the top of a house, that was primarily designed as a look-out. A gazebo, on the other hand, is strictly a garden building, is enclosed on three sides and is more akin to a summerhouse. It would be comfortably furnished, with furniture and floor coverings, and would serve, literally, as a summer house. Today's gazebo, however, looks more like a large-scale arbour, except that it's likely to be decorative in its own right and substantial enough to provide a degree of shade and privacy without having to be smothered with climbing plants.

All these structures can be a real boon to outdoor living, providing a permanent setting for leisure activities and relaxation and offering a certain amount of protection against the elements. But they play an invaluable role in terms of design, too, by introducing a vertical element into the garden and at the same time providing interest at eye level. This can also be achieved with the simplest of devices, the archway. No matter how basic or ornate, position an arch correctly – to frame a focal point, say, or to encourage exploration of a particular area of the lawn – and it will work wonders.

A final thought on the subject of overhead structures. While it's obviously desirable to have one area of the garden that is shaded from the midday sun, consider the well-being of your lawn before getting too carried away. We might want to turn our lawn into an outdoor room but that doesn't mean we want a solid roof! Materials and plants that are to be pressed into action for overhead shelter should be chosen with care and used judiciously so as to let enough light through. Where heavy or constant shade is unavoidable, make sure you sow or turf the area with a suitably tolerant variety of grass. And if you opt to fix permanent plastic sheeting to the roof of the pergola to provide shelter from rain (see 'Setting the scene – Against the elements'), remember that you'll have to water on a regular basis to keep that area of lawn healthy and verdant.

Overleaf: The clean, geometric lines of these sophisticated trellis panels make a bold statement, and the theme is continued in the modern choice of paving materials for a path

85

Today's garden designers are coming up with increasingly imaginative ideas, applying a modern approach to traditional materials – this garden arch is striking enough to stand alone, needing no further adornment in the way of plants

Dividing lines

Every garden, however small, will benefit from the addition of some form of screening. At its most practical it may be used to provide shelter from wind or privacy from neighbours but it can also be used simply to set a certain mood or create a feeling of intimacy. In all cases, paying attention to details of design is vital if you are to achieve a visually appealing result.

The smaller your garden, the less you will want a screen that looks too solid or imposing. Obviously all structures have to be stable and reasonably robust but in confined spaces you need a screen that is relatively light and airy in appearance, otherwise the effect could be claustrophobic. To the same end, you should use screening judiciously – you don't want a lawn composed of cubicles – and keep it fairly low. For most purposes, screens at eye-level are perfectly adequate.

Solid walls, unless they are very low, and close-boarded fences are best kept to the perimeter of your garden. And even here you should bear in mind that an inpenetrable surface isn't a prerequisite for either shelter or privacy. Generally, the most effective

88

windbreak is a structure that filters the wind, not blocks it out –
this can cause severe buffeting and unpleasant eddies – and, very
often, one that simply gives an impression of privacy is all that is
needed.

Whatever form of screening you choose it will need to be
securely anchored. Usually that will involve the sinking of stout
timber uprights into the ground, maybe to a depth of 18in or 2ft
depending on the height and weight of the screen, either bedding
them into concrete or using a proprietary anchoring device. If the
design you choose demands cross-rails, make sure that these too
are sufficiently robust and are firmly fixed to the uprights. Any
wood will need to be treated with a suitable preservative, of
course, but you can minimise the risk of rotting by keeping the
screen itself clear of the ground.

There's no shortage of off-the-shelf screens to choose from.
Some are so sophisticated and attractive that they need no further
adornment in the way of plants and you can let the beauty of the
structures speak for themselves. Styles range from the intricately
ornate and traditional to the bold geometric and contemporary. At
their best they are craftsman-made from quality materials and, not
surprisingly, are rather expensive. Increasingly imaginative mass-
produced lines are becoming more widely available, though,
which will do the job and look good without costing you the earth.

There's much to be said for the traditional timber trellis panels,
however. They can look extremely attractive – especially if finished
with a coloured wood stain to make them more individual – and
they are highly affordable. Square trellis designs can even be cut
into to create an unusual staggered top edge. Or you could create
charming peep-holes by carefully cutting away sections within the
panel. The addition of climbing plants is going to be imperative if
you want shelter and privacy, of course, but for a purely visual
division the trellis can be left simple and bare.

If you're willing to do-it-yourself you can cut costs and create
superbly original screening, and you don't need an A-level in
carpentry. Using a basic framework of uprights and cross-rails, you
can create any number of imaginative screen designs using
arrangements of timber slats or even bamboos or wattle hurdles.
Again, subtle or striking combinations of coloured wood stains
can be pressed into action to enhance the timber and reinforce
the individuality of your design.

Not yet mentioned is how screens can be used as camouflage.
While your lawn may be set aside for relaxation and entertainment,
the rest of the garden might well have to work for a living and that
means compost bins, sheds, incinerators and so forth. Apart from
the fact that these aren't the most attractive of items, the last thing
you want is a constant reminder of the chores awaiting you. The
answer? Simply hide them away behind a decorative screen and
what the eye doesn't see . . .!

This only serves to re-emphasise the fact that the majority of
permanent structures are best built, or at the very least allocated
a site, before you even begin to think about making or re-shaping
your lawn. And then, as you will see from the plan at the end of
this chapter, it takes only a little common sense to create a garden
where that lawn will work for you!

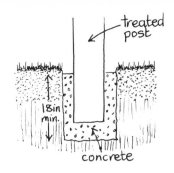

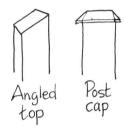

Angled top *Post cap*

*However lightweight the screen, the
supporting posts will need to be
securely anchored in the ground. Use
post caps or an angled cut so that
rainwater runs away easily*

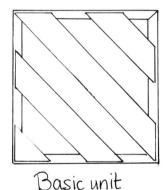

Basic unit

*Basic slatted units like this can make
highly effective screens when
combined to form different patterns –
diagonals, zig-zags or diamonds, for
example. Similar screening systems
are available from several
manufacturers*

The gazebo alone would be a superb
focal point but combined with a stylish
seat and positioned in a shady corner,
partly hidden, the effect is stunning
and irresistibly intriguing

A basic arbour frame, brightly painted,
can be used to create a pleasing
feature with instant effect – a useful
ploy while waiting for climbers to
smother the structure

Permanent features like a pergola help to set a particular mood, giving the garden immediate character, and provide a structural backbone that can be used to link plantings and other items to create an harmonious effect

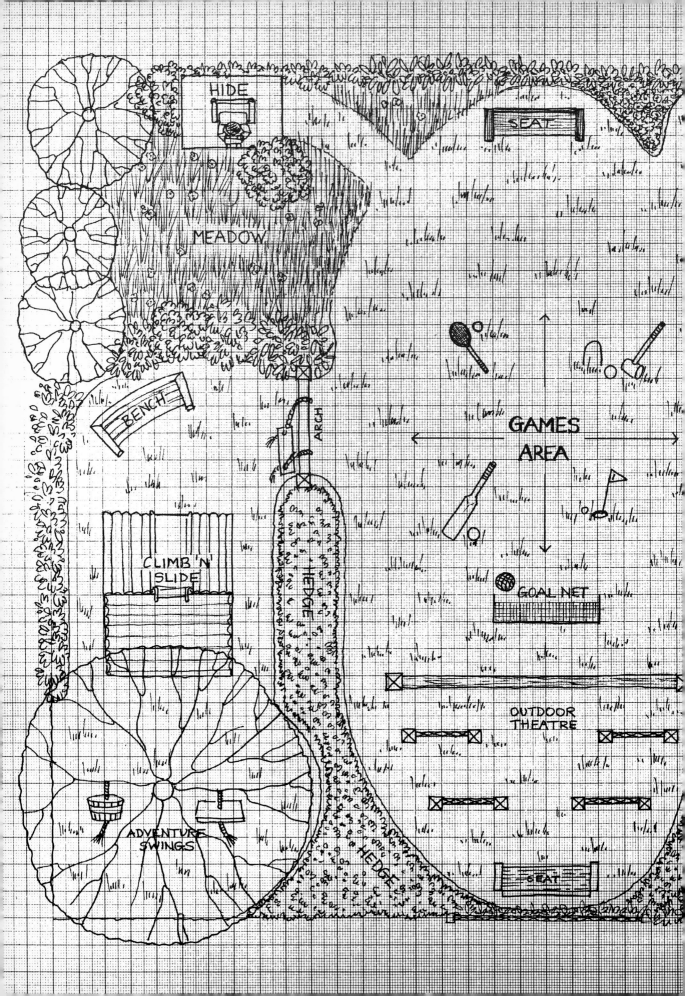

HIDE

SEAT

MEADOW

BENCH

ARCH

GAMES AREA

CLIMB 'N' SLIDE

HEDGE

GOAL NET

OUTDOOR THEATRE

ADVENTURE SWINGS

HEDGE

SEAT

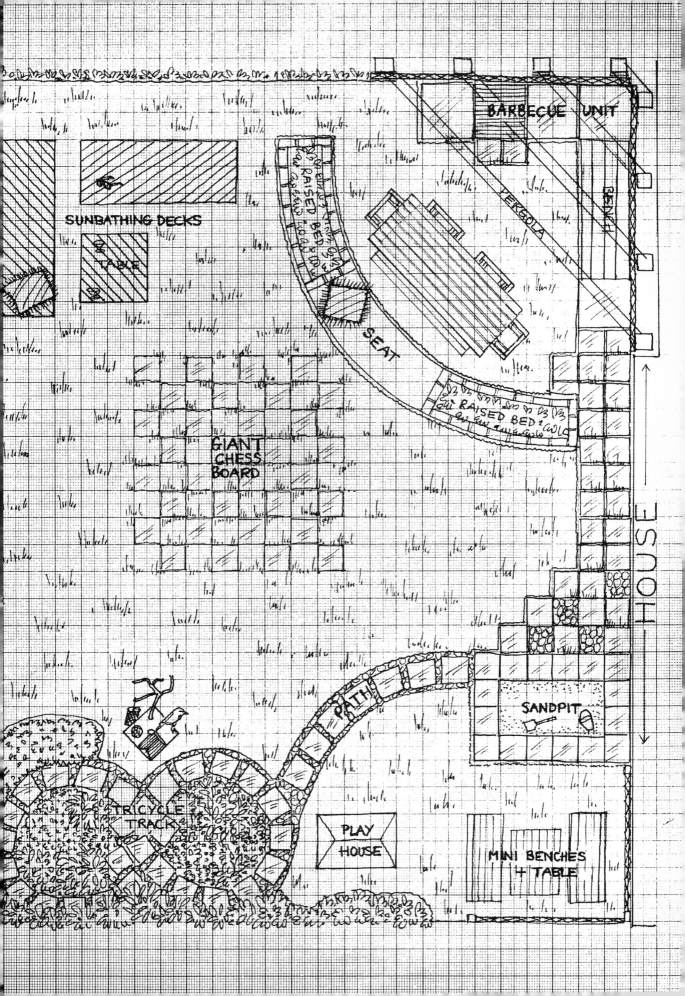

APPENDIX

PRODUCT INFORMATION
Manufacturers whose products are illustrated

Barrel-Play Ltd:
The Vineyard, Sherston, Nr Malmesbury,
Wilts SN16 0PY
Tel: 0666 840141
Pages 15, 22 (bottom), 23 (bottom)

Barlow Tyrie Ltd:
Braintree, Essex CM7 7RN
Tel: 0376 22505
Page 66

Andrew Crace Designs:
Bourne Lane, Much Hadham, Herts SG10 6ER
Tel: 0279 84 2685
Pages 54 (bottom), 55 (top), 90 (top)

Dovetail Services:
Unit D18, Barwell Trading Estate,
Leatherhead Road, Chessington,
Surrey KT9 2NW
Tel: 01 974 1115
Page 47

Harlequin:
Derwent Designs Ltd, Crambe Grange,
Barton-le-Willows, York YO6 7PD
Tel: 065 381 210/8112
Page 55 (bottom)

John Jaques & Son Ltd:
361 Whitehorse Road, Thornton Heath,
Surrey CR4 8XP
Tel: 01 684 4242
Pages 42 (bottom), 46

Machin Designs Ltd:
Ransome's Dock, Parkgate Road,
London SW11 4NP
Tel: 01 350 1581
Page 54 (top)

MY Sports & Games Ltd:
154 Wharfdale Road, Tyseley,
Birmingham B11 2DG
Tel: 021 706 9010
Pages 30 (top), 34 (left)

Practical Products Ltd:
39 Verran Road, Camberley, Surrey GU15 2ND
Tel: 0276 62722
Page 67

Roseney Farm Designs:
Lanlivery, Bodmin, Cornwall PL30 5DL
Tel: 0208 872664
Page 51

Stuart Garden Architecture:
Barrington Court, Barrington, Ilminster,
Somerset TA1 0NQ
Tel: 0460 42003
Page 86

TP Activity Toys:
Tube Plastics Ltd, Severn Road,
Stourport-on-Severn, Worcestershire
Tel: 0299 827728
Pages 14, 23 (centre), 26 (bottom), 27, 30 (bottom), 31

Flymo Ltd
For further information on Flymo products and details of your local stockist, contact: Customer Service Department, Flymo Ltd, Hurworth Road, Aycliffe Industrial Estate, Newton Aycliffe, County Durham DL5 6UP. Tel: 0325 315161

Other useful addresses
Denavie:
21 Kirkview Crescent, Newton Mearns, Glasgow G77 5DB – handmade bowls and skittles

Hillian Interlog Ltd:
Eagle House, Oakwood Lane, Port Talbot, East Glamorgan SA13 1DF – self-assembly timber sandpit/pool, tree seat

Kwik Cricket Ltd:
c/o The Cricket Council, Lord's Cricket Ground, FREEPOST, London NW8 0YP – Kwik Cricket information, brochure, order forms for kits

Lotus Water Garden Products:
260–300 Berkhampstead Road, Chesham, Bucks HP5 3EZ – pools, fountains, plants and accessories

Premier Boule Supplies:
Midwood, Benenden Road, Biddenden, Ashford, Kent TN27 8BY – suppliers of boules and accessories

Stapeley Water Gardens Ltd:
Stapeley, Nantwich, Cheshire CW5 7LH – pools, fountains, plants and accessories

The Leisure and Outdoor Furniture Association:
60 Claremont Road, Surbiton, Surrey KT6 4RH – for information and advice on choosing and caring for garden furniture and barbecues

All the above information was correct at the time of going to press.

FURTHER READING

Baines, Chris. **The Wild Side of Town** (BBC Publications/Elm Tree Books)
Edden, Gill. **The Garden Handyman** (Black Cat/Macdonald)
Freeman, Garth. **Pétanque – The French Game of Boules** (The Carreau Press)
Hessayon, Dr D. G. **The Lawn Expert** (pbi Publications)
Palin, Robert. **The Master Gardener's Guide to Lawn Care** (Salamander Books)

The publishers wish to thank *Practical Gardening* magazine for permission to use the photographs on pages 6, 70; and Jim Deen for the photograph on page 43. Grateful acknowledgement is also made to *Garden Answers* magazine for permission to reproduce Carol Kurrein's illustrations on pages 16 (top), 19 (top left), 58 (below), 80, 82, 83, 88, 90, and the photograph on page 91. The illustrations on pages 41 and 47 are from The Mary Evans Picture Library.
The publishers also gratefully acknowledge the co-operation of those manufacturers and suppliers who provided photographs for the book (see Product Information).
Permission to quote from the following published works is gratefully acknowledged: *Kilvert's Diary* (edited by William Plomer) by courtesy of Mrs Sheila Hooper and Jonathan Cape Ltd; *The Wild Side of Town* by Chris Baines, published by BBC Publications/Elm Tree Books at £10.95, by courtesy of Hamish Hamilton Ltd.

Kurrein, Carol.   636
    The Flymo book of garden games   K79
and lawn leisure.

Date Due

FEB 0 2 1993			
JUL 7 1994			

BRODART, INC.   Cat. No. 23 233   Printed in U.S.A.